MEL BAY PRESENTS

MARK O'CON

The Championship Years

1975-1984

Transcribed and Edited by
Stacy Phillips with Mark O'Connor

Contents

Introduction

A stroke of good fortune placed a child prodigy, Mark O'Connor, and a creative master fiddler, Benny Thomasson, in a small town in Idaho in 1973. The latter had the temperament to share his deep understanding of creativity in the context of traditional, old-time fiddling; the former had a burning desire to emulate his teacher. Some of the wonderful story of the friendship between Mark and Benny is related in **"Conversation with Mark O'Connor"** later in this book. In a sense the music in this compilation and the accompanying album of the same name (Country Music Foundation 015) is their gift.

Specifically, this book shows how Mark took what he learned from Benny and produced an original voice in fiddle tune variation, becoming the most celebrated fiddler of the late '70s through '80s.

Mark burst into the fiddle world as a precociously gifted player, upon winning the Junior Division of the prestigious Weiser National Oldtime Fiddlers' Contest on his first attempt. It was immediately obvious that his talent was something special — great tone, drive, imagination, and inspiration, especially considering his age. He became the major force in developing a "national" fiddle style and boosting fiddle contests to new heights of popularity — all by the time he was 19 years old. Yet his first professional job was playing **guitar** with the David Grisman Quintet. He also became an outstanding mandolin player.

After leaving Grisman, Mark played fiddle with one of the hottest rock-fusion bands ever, The Dregs. Following the breakup of that group he gradually worked himself into the position of the preeminent Nashville country studio fiddler. So, in the space of about 15 years Mark has performed with unequivocal success at the highest levels of four music styles: old-time fiddling, string-band jazz, rock, and commercial country.

Meanwhile he has been developing a personal music statement, reflected in his recent solo albums.

This book contains meticulously accurate transcriptions of the music on the album *Mark O'Connor—The Championship Years*. It details the first phase of Mark's career, during which he established a new standard for old-time fiddling. All the tunes were performed at the Weiser, Idaho, fiddle contest. In its Open Division, each contestant must play six rounds of three tunes apiece. Each round requires a hoedown (or hornpipe), a waltz, and a tune-of-choice. The latter can include all the other categories of fiddle tunes such as jigs, schottisches, or any unidentifiable genre. Mark's choices usually were rags or polkas. The transcriptions fit these groupings as follows:

Hoedowns and Hornpipes

1. Grey Eagle
2. Dusty Miller
3. Sally Goodwin
4. Tom and Jerry
5. Billy in the Lowground
6. Sally Johnson
7. Brilliancy
8. Leather Britches
9. Golden Eagle Hornpipe
10. Tugboat
11. Hell Among the Yearlings
12. Bill Cheatum
13. Choctaw
14. Herman's Hornpipe
15. Sally Ann
16. Arkansas Traveller

Waltzes

1. Yellow Rose
2. Wednesday Night
3. Westphalia

Tunes-of-Choice

1. Grandfather Polka
2. I Don't Love Nobody
3. Herman's Rag
4. Allentown Polka
5. Black and White Rag
6. Dill Pickle Rag
7. Don't Let the Deal Go Down
8. Beaumont Rag
9. Jesse Polka

Several of these titles are presented more than once, with different arrangements and even keys to exhibit Mark's musical growth, stimulated by his continuing challenges to himself.

Mark O'Connor and Stacy Phillips   *(Photo by Jim McGuire)*

Acknowledgments

Mark wishes to acknowledge the following fiddlers:

"My primary influence was Benny Thomasson. My fiddle teachers were Barbara Lamb and John Burke. Thanks to the following fiddlers who made an impact on my music: Kenny Baker, Dick Barrett, Byron Berline, Loretta Brank, J. C. Broughton, Orville Burns, James Chancellor (Texas Shorty), Vassar Clements, Roy Lee Cowan, Junior Daugherty, Major Franklin, Johnny Gimble, Stephane Grappelli, Herman Johnson, Clark Kessinger, Terry Morris, Buddy Pendleton, J. T. Perkins, Jean-Luc Ponty, Eck Robertson, Norman Solomon, Vernon Solomon, Buddy Spicher, Joe Venuti, and Bob Wills."

We also wish to thank:

Kyle Young of the Country Music Foundation

William Bay and Dean Bye of Mel Bay Publications

Judy Parsons of the Weiser Chamber of Commerce

Andrea Zonn for assisting in the proofreading of the music

Michelle O'Connor

Matt Glaser

Lyle Reed for making his original recordings available

Unless otherwise indicated, the photos are from Mark O'Connor's personal collection. Most of them were photographed by his mother, Martha O'Connor.

The National Oldtime Fiddlers' Contest at Weiser

Weiser, Idaho, is a small town located on the Oregon–Idaho border. During the third full week of June, it is transformed into the "fiddling capitol of the world," with seven different age and status categories being decided.

Fiddle contests were held in Weiser as early as 1914, but the current version of the competition began in 1953. In the mid-1960s its prestige began to grow, and now it is among the three or four premier fiddle events in America.

Among the famous players to win one of its various divisions are: Clark Kessinger, Byron Berline, Lu Berline (father of Byron), Frazier Moss, Benny Thomasson, Sam Bush and, of course, Mark O'Connor.

National Grand Champions at Weiser
(This designation was established in 1963.)

1963	Lloyd Wanzer
1964	Cleo Persinger
1965	Byron Berline
1966	Cyril Stinnett
1967	Lloyd Wanzer
1968	Herman Johnson
1969	Herman Johnson
1970	Byron Berline
1971	Dick Barrett
1972	Dick Barrett
1973	Herman Johnson
1974	Benny Thomasson
1975	Dick Barrett
1976	Dick Barrett
1977	Herman Johnson
1978	Herman Johnson
1979	Mark O'Connor
1980	Mark O'Connor
1981	Mark O'Connor
1982	John Francis
1983	Tony Ludiker
1984	Mark O'Connor
1985	Dale Morris Jr.
1986	Randy Pollard
1987	Jimmie Don Bates
1988	Matthew Hartz
1989	Tony Ludiker
1990	Rudi Booher

NATIONAL OLDTIME FIDDLERS' CONTEST

Weiser, Idaho 83672

Third Full Week in June

GENERAL CONTEST RULES
Amended 1989

(Apply to National Grand Champion, Senior, Men, Ladies, Junior, Junior-Junior, Small Fry Contests)

1. Entry blank must be completed and entry fee paid before June 1 to avoid late fee. We need pre-registrations to more effectively run the program. Money will be refunded to anyone who paid entry fee and cannot attend, if they inform the committee of withdrawal prior to the contest's beginning.

2. All commercial recording rights are reserved and shall become the property of the Weiser Chamber of Commerce, the non-profit and legal entity for the National Oldtime Fiddlers' Contest Committee. Signing of registration for the Contest shall waive such rights.

3. The fiddle committee officials will randomly select the initial order of appearance for the first preliminary round. Judging Chairman in future rounds will draw before each round for new order of appearance. Announcements will be made of the drawings, and contestants must be ready to play when called. Any contestant registered and not playing will be eliminated from next year's Contest. Contestant's badge and guest badge will be revoked for remainder of this year's Contest. Any contestant who harasses or threatens a judge will be automatically eliminated for the current Contest and next year's Contest.

4. Any accompanist registered and not accompanying a contesting fiddler (excluding the Certified Contest) on stage will not be allowed to register as an accompanist for next year's Contest.

5. Contestants at each appearance must first play a hoedown; second, a waltz, and third, a tune of their choice **other than** a hoedown or waltz. No tune shall be played more than once during all appearances of a contestant. Four minute playing time will be strictly adhered to. Ten points will be deducted from total score for each 30 second interval or portion thereof.

6. If a string breaks, the FIDDLER will have the option to continue or stop at that point. If the tune is completed it will be judged as played. If the fiddler stops play he will be allowed to begin with that tune and complete his program.

7. Contestants may play without accompanist or with not more than two, but may register only one.

8. Any danceable folk tunes played in oldtime fiddle fashion are acceptable.

9. Contact microphones and amplified instruments will not be permitted.

10. No trick or fancy fiddling allowed during the contesting appearances. No cross tuning on stage.

11. No sheet music shall be displayed in the contesting area.

12. Judging will be scored for oldtime fiddling ability, danceability, rhythm or timing, and tone quality. Scores will be accumulative. Points will be deducted for any violation of the above rules, No. 4 through 10 (inclusive).

13. Any contestant winning three consecutive years in the Grand National Division must either judge next year's Contest or sit out the next year's Contest.

14. Any contestant winning three consecutive years in the Senior, Men, Ladies, and Junior divisions automatically move into the Grand National Division. Any Junior-Junior winning three consecutive times will automatically move into the Junior Division. Any Small Fry winning three consecutive times will automatically move into the Junior-Junior Division.

15. Any contestant winning a trophy or money must appear on stage to receive their awards or this trophy and money will be forfeited.

16. Any protest must be submitted in writing to the Contest Chairman, and signed by not less than three contestants of the Contest involved within three hours of protest occurrence.

17. All decisions of the Judges and of the Contest Committee will be final.

SPECIAL CONTEST RULES
Contestants may enter only one of the following contests:

NATIONAL:	1. Contestants, open to all regardless of age.	**6 Rounds**
	2. Contestants may be of either sex.	
SENIOR:	1. Contestants must be at least 65 years of age.	**4 Rounds**
	2. Contestants may be of either sex.	
MEN:	1. Contestants must be at least 18 years of age.	**4 Rounds**
	2. Contestants — Men only.	
LADIES:	1. Contestants must be at least 18 years of age.	**4 Rounds**
	2. Contestants — Ladies only.	
JUNIOR:	1. Contestants must be less than 18 years of age.	**4 Rounds**
	2. Contestants may be of either sex.	
JUNIOR-JUNIOR:	1. Contestants must be less than 13 years of age.	**3 Rounds**
	2. Contestants may be of either sex.	
SMALL FRY:	1. Contestants must be less than 9 years of age.	**3 Rounds**
	2. Contestants may be of either sex.	

Schedule of Events

Sunday, June 17, 1990 —

12:00 p.m.—Registration of fiddlers begins in High School lobby.

4:00 p.m.—General meeting of Contest Committee with all fiddlers in auditorium, General Chairman conducting.

Monday, June 18, 1990 —

7:30 a.m.—Registration of fiddlers in High School lobby.

8:00 a.m.—Ladies Round One followed by Small Fry followed by Ladies Round Two.

7:30 p.m.—Pre-Program Jam Session on stage by California State Fiddlers.

8:00 p.m.—Invocation — Pastor David Thorne, Riverside Baptist Church.
Introduction of Judges.
National Ladies Semi-Finals and Finals.
Certified Contest — These are winners from area certified contests that are Small Fry and Junior-Juniors. There will be four awards presented to these contest winners based on best fiddling, fanciest fiddling, and fanciest dressed fiddlers — male and female.
Awards presented by Tammy Gibson, Miss Washington County.

Tuesday, June 19, 1990 —

7:30 a.m.—Registration of fiddlers in High School lobby.

8:00 a.m.—Junior-Junior Preliminary followed by Small Fry Preliminary.

7:00 p.m.—Special by Arizona Fiddlers.

7:30 p.m.—Pre-Program Jam Session on stage by California State Fiddlers.

8:00 p.m.—Invocation — Pastor Dick Scott, First Christian Church.
Introduction of Judges.
Introduction of previous night's winners.
National Junior-Junior and Small Fry Semi-Finals and Finals.
Youngest competing contestant award.
Certified Contest — These are winners from area certified contests that are Seniors and Juniors. There will be four awards presented to these regional contest winners based on best fiddling, fanciest fiddling, and fanciest dressed fiddlers — male and female.
Awards presented by Tammy Gibson, Miss Washington County.

Wednesday, June 20, 1990 —

7:30 a.m.—Registration of fiddlers in High School lobby.

8:00 a.m.—Junior Preliminary followed by National Grand Champion followed by Junior Second Round.

7:00 p.m.—Specials.

7:30 p.m.—Pre-Program Jam Session on stage by California State Fiddlers.

8:00 p.m.—Invocation — Pastor Emory Macy, Advent Christian Church.
Introduction of Judges.
Introduction of previous night's winners.
Junior Semi-Finals and Finals.
Certified Contest — These are winners from area certified contests that are Ladies, Men's, and Grand Champions. There will be four awards presented to these regional contest winners based on best fiddling, fanciest fiddling, and fanciest dressed fiddlers — male and female.
Awards presented by Tammy Gibson, Miss Washington County.

Thursday, June 21, 1990 —

7:30 a.m.—Registration of fiddlers in High School lobby.

8:00 a.m.—Men's Preliminary followed by National Grand Champion Second Preliminary followed by Men's Round Two.

7:00 p.m.—Specials.

7:30 p.m.—Pre-Program Jam Session on stage by California State Fiddlers.

8:00 p.m.—Invocation — Pastor Lloyd Barney, Calvary Baptist Chapel.
Introduction of Judges.
Introduction of previous night's winners.
Men's Semi-Finals and Finals.
Awards presented by Tammy Gibson, Miss Washington County.

Friday, June 22, 1990 —

8:00 a.m.—Senior Round One followed by National Grand Champion. Seniors Second Preliminary followed by National Grand Champion Third Preliminary.

7:00 p.m.—Specials.

7:30 p.m.—Pre-Program Jam Session on stage by California State Fiddlers.

8:00 p.m.—Invocation — Pastor Jim Powell, Weiser Assembly of God.
Introduction of Judges.
Introduction of previous night's winners.
National Grand Champion Preliminary and Senior Finals.
Awards presented by Tammy Gibson, Miss Washington County.

Senior Citizens 65 years and older admitted free during daytime contesting Friday.

Saturday, June 23, 1990 —

8:00 a.m.—Fiddlers Golf Tournament.

11:00 a.m.—Parade entries form at Junior High under direction of parade chairman.

12:00 noon—Parade to commence and will tour downtown business area.
Jaycee Barbecue following parade at City Park.
Four County Art Guild, art in the park.

2:00 p.m.—Jam Session at Hall of Fame, 10 East Idaho.

7:00 p.m.—Specials.

7:30 p.m.—Pre-Program Jam Session on stage by California State Fiddlers.

8:00 p.m.—Invocation — Pastor Keith Sargent, Oasis Christian Book Store.
Introduction of Judges.
Introduction of previous night's winners.
National Grand Champion Finals. Awards will be presented to the top National Finalists.
Awards presented to the accompanists will be made during the program and cash awards will be made to the top winners at the end of the program by Tammy Gibson, Miss Washington County.

Schedule of events at the 1990 edition of the Weiser contest

Contestant No. _____

NATIONAL OLDTIME FIDDLERS' CONTEST®
Weiser, Idaho

_____ Round   June ____, 19____   Contest _____

POSSIBLE POINTS	Danceability 25%	Oldtime Style 25%	Rhythm 25%	Tone 25%	TOTAL 100%
1. Hoedown					
2. Waltz					
3. Tune of Choice					
				GRAND TOTAL	

Judge _____

Judge's scoring sheet

Conversation with Mark O'Connor

While checking my transcriptions for errors, Mark and I had a meandering conversation over a two-day period. I wanted to know what it was like being a nationally known fiddler while dealing with being a teenager in the Seattle, Washington area.

[The three-dot notation (. . .) refers to pauses in the ebb and flow of conversation and not, as is usual, to portions of the quotes that have been omitted.]

Stacy Phillips: What kind of reputation did you have at school?

Mark O'Connor: Terrible. Anything dealing with music at this time was a bummer. The music I was playing was too different for them [fellow students] to accept as normal. For a kid, not normal is a bad situation. I wasn't into going to the drag races. I didn't do team sports much, though I liked basketball the best. I didn't like to go to rock concerts. I like to now, much more than when I was a teenager.

The only socializing I did was through skateboarding [at the ages of approximately 14–17]. My emphasis shifted from doing music all the time. It wasn't only good exercise and fun, but it helped me hang out with my peers. There were one or two rock-and-roll guys that I formed a rock fusion band with as a senior.

SP: Playing guitar?

MO: Yes. Before that I had a hard time. Every time I'd get written up in the newspaper, some teacher would put it on the bulletin board. That would be my nightmare. The teacher thought it was neat. The kids threw darts at it.

SP: You'd be wearing a cowboy hat in the picture?

MO: Living in Seattle, wearing a cowboy hat was not the hippest thing. Everyone was into flared jeans and clodhoppers, kind of mountain shoes.

SP: Then you were leading a bit of a double life, trying to keep them separate.

MO: Almost a double personality . . . in order to survive because my school was rough. You might think that a talented kid would go to a special school. I couldn't get any time off to improve my musical education.

SP: So you tried to hide that part of your life?

MO: Tried. I had a real problem. I was a big target. I would never play fiddle at school. They would have laughed. The one thing I really regret is not being in an environment where that would be appreciated. There are areas where that would have been well accepted. We couldn't afford another school. It was all we could do to travel to contests in the summer.

SP: Where did you go?

MO: The Grand Masters in Nashville.

SP: That's a long way.

MO: We'd stop over on the way. I ended up flying a lot to the Grand Masters because Weiser was the next week. So I came there by myself several times.

That was the beginning of my summer. We'd end up coming to Nashville later on in the summer. I'd fly down and stay with friends and fly back and drive to Weiser. From Weiser we'd take off to the whole contest circuit. We'd look at a schedule. There were some favorites we'd always come back to. One was in Ogden, Utah, others in Northern California and New Mexico. Another in Kentucky, Memphis, Tulsa, Oklahoma, and Langley, Oklahoma. Also Denver, Nebraska, and Winfield, Kansas, every year.

I didn't go to many in Texas because most of the time only Texans were allowed. I went to Crockett and El Paso.

June 1976: Michelle took third in the Junior-Juniors, and Mark won the Juniors.

SP: Who went with you?

MO: Usually my mom and sister [Michelle]. My sister played some, too. I probably averaged 15 contests during the summer. There were a couple of local ones in the winter.

SP: Can you imagine entering again?

MO: No, I've got too much of a professional reputation now. Back then it was perfect. I was a student and it was my only outlet. I was too young to play in clubs and I didn't have the chance to play too many concerts. It was my only chance to play in front of a lot of people. I had this instrument and I was progressing. **Now** what do I do? You go to local state contests and then you go to Weiser. Later on I realized I had a chance to win major events. When I was a kid I wasn't serious about it. I was doing it for fun. I did have a record out when I was 12 [*National Junior Fiddle Champion* on Rounder Records].

I wasn't old enough to care a great deal about the outcome. That's probably why my playing was so carefree, like "Billy in the Lowground," being as crazy as I felt like.

SP: This was when you competed in the Junior Division at Weiser?

MO: Yes.

SP: Who was winning the Open those years?

MO: Herman Johnson, Dick Barrett. When I competed in the Open I realized I could win, and that started to be my purpose for going. Before that it was to learn more. When I was a kid the emphasis was equally on doing well in the contest, but equal to that was learning from older fiddlers, being a kid, and getting a vacation out of the deal. Later, when I was 17–19 I took it more seriously.

SP: How many years did you travel to contests with your family?

MO: 1974–'79. That was the year I went with David Grisman's Quintet and I arrived at Weiser from San Francisco.

SP: That was your first full-time professional job?

MO: Yes. I was 17. I was with him a year and a half.

SP: Did you go directly to The Dregs after that?

MO: Yeah, for another year and a half.

From there it was a searching time. I did miscellaneous jobs for about 2½ years. I lived in Atlanta a year longer and went to a lot of contests around the South to help pay rent. Then I moved to Nashville in 1983 to try and break into sessions. I entered contests in Kentucky, Tennessee, and Alabama.

SP: How did you know where the contests were?

MO: If I went to one contest, that's where I would get information. "Are you going to Clarkesville?" "Where's that?"

SP: When I saw you in Nashville during that time, you were playing at the Bluebird [a music club away from the tourist scene].

MO: Thirty dollars for a night.

SP: You had to prove yourself to a different set of people.

MO: For about 1½ years it was touch and go. In '85 I broke through. I can narrow it down to two performances on albums. The Nitty Gritty Dirt Band called me for a song called "High Horse." I had played some shows with John McEuen [one-time banjoist with the Dirt Band]. When they moved to Nashville to play country music instead of rock, they called me.

Within a couple of months Michael Murphy did a country album. He knew my guitar and fiddle playing. He wrote this song called "The Fiddling Man." He wanted me even though I was untested in recording sessions. Both these were with the heavyweight session players. They both made it onto the radio. [This was in 1985.]

SP: Meanwhile you were playing with. . . ?

MO: Peter Rowan, John McEuen, and Doc Watson were my primary work.

SP: On that folk scene, people were aware of you, but that doesn't count in the Nashville scene. You're nowhere if you play bluegrass. Is that a fair statement?

MO: Yes. I didn't really know how to play on sessions. I just knew that I was talented. If I feel like playing a certain way one day I'll just do that because that's the only thing I can really trust myself on. If I tried to imitate another session fiddler, it might be, in my worst nightmare, a terrible imitation. If I blew it I would never forgive myself. I went in and played the way I felt I should play on that song. Like on "High Horse" they didn't tell me what to play. I basically said, "Here's how I play." They said, "We like that. We never heard anything like that before."

I was in and out of the "High Horse" session in 20 minutes. The session was at 2:00. John McEuen strolls in at 2:20 and he says [in a concerned tone], "Mark hasn't shown up yet." They tell him, "He's been here and gone!" Second take.

SP: It's a big plus to be able to knock them off like that.

MO: I felt that if I was going to have any chance, I would have to create a new sound. Plus, if I was going to enjoy it at all, it would have to be me doing what I enjoy.

Now people call because they like what I've done. It's almost like having to prove myself every time I step into the studio, but I do have a reputation. "If Mark can do anything like he did on this other record, I'll be happy."

It was touch and go at the beginning. When I came to Nashville in '83, I would listen to country radio to see what was happening, and I would hear a fiddle maybe every 15 or 20 songs! I'm going, "Maybe there just ain't that much to do." It was scary. It was the Kenny Rogers era . . . really middle-of-the-road stuff. Right now there's a fiddle buzz here. Every band has a fiddler and almost every record has one. Even the pop acts like Sawyer Brown and James Taylor-type singer songwriters.

No one in the industry knows who won the Grand Masters. But winning did help me. I took it one step further and was a celebrated winner. I was doing other things, I wasn't just a contest player.

When I came to Nashville, I was more known for playing with The Dregs than my contest things. They made such an impact here when they played, though the gig was with their other fiddler [Alan Sloan]. They thought that anyone who played in that group must be good.

SP: The guys who win at Weiser and the Grand Masters must play in local country or Western swing bands in their home towns.

MO: Right.

SP: Please talk about how you met and then learned from Benny Thomasson.

MO: When I was growing up in Seattle, there were plenty of amateur musicians to learn from and there were a couple of greats. When I heard Benny Thomasson, it was a revelation. The first thing I thought was, "I didn't know that's possible." I didn't know that fiddle music could sound that great.

Mark's first year at Weiser, participating in the parade, June 1973.

I had seen Doug Kershaw on TV, a wild and crazy fiddler. That's what got me enthused about playing fiddle. I thought that fiddling was really happening, "I want to do that." But when I saw Benny Thomasson play old-time fiddle, even back then I knew it was the neatest thing. Even today it holds true.

The first year I went to Weiser, my first fiddle teacher, Barbara Lamb . . . her goal was to get me far enough along to where I could compete in the Junior-Junior Division, 12 and under competition. It was about a ten-hour drive there. More importantly, it was a chance to see some really great fiddlers, one of them being Benny Thomasson, who we learned had moved to Washington State about two hours from Seattle. He moved there to be closer to one of his sons. Also, the climate suited his health and he liked the fishing. He was going to retire from music. The local folk society found out about him, and he influenced my whole generation of fiddlers in the Northwest.

SP: He made the Northwest a hotbed of fiddling.

MO: Right. He had lots of patience to teach, and he was an inspirational character. You wanted to emulate him.

SP: Talk about his place in the fiddle world.

MO: Right away some things come to mind. Every old tune he played he rearranged. He wasn't a composer in the sense that he made up new tunes. He reworked the old tunes, and in that sense he was very much a composer. He would compose variations and, in his words, "round out" the tunes. For lack of a better term, he would make them a bit more virtuosic.

Part of it was that he was a natural player. His bowing was the smoothest ever and his phrasing . . . I think Benny's fiddle phrasing is like George Jones' vocal phrasing. Every time George Jones opens his mouth, you might as well write it in stone. It's not going to get much better than that. Everything he does is classic.

So here was Benny, 64 years old when I met him, and I was 11, and we started an amazing friendship. Who would have known that an 11-year-old boy would hang out with him and we would befriend each other. I went down to his house a lot.

SP: You weren't just his student. There was something more there.

MO: Yeah, he kind of looked after me.

SP: I see it as an American version of an Indian guru and his disciple.

MO: He saw that I had the ability to make up my own variations, even though I thought that everything he played was exactly what I wanted to do. He would teach me his exact notes if I wanted, but he would say, "Now, Mark, you could make this even better." What he meant was that he knew that I probably had the talent. He encouraged me. He would open up by going, "You can do it like this or do it like that, because I don't have an exact, set way to do it."

He was very humble. It gave me confidence because here is a person playing something so overwhelming that, on my own, I just wouldn't think of changing. In my mind there was no way it could be better. By saying, "You could rework it for yourself and it would be better" . . . that encouragement was enough to make me explore my own boundaries. Con-

16

Twelve-year-old Mark O'Connor learning all he can from Benny Thomasson at the latter's house in Kalama, Washington, December 1973.

sequently, when I was 13 and 14, I developed my own variations, even though I got the substance of the music from him.

He'd want to hear my variations. That was part of the lesson. I didn't have a set lesson with him. I'd spend a couple of days at a time with him, and I'd learn maybe 5 tunes a day. I couldn't play them up to speed, but I got the gist and I'd tape them. Then I'd be set for the next several weeks. Then I'd come down for another 5 or 10 tunes. I learned like 200 songs over a couple of years.

SP: Can you think of some rare ones?

MO: One in particular, I think was called "Big Chief Sitting in the Rain." I was really more interested in learning the standards. The thing to do was to learn the songs everybody played, but do them better. My approach to fiddling was, I wanted to play "Sally Goodin" and make a rendition that's better. That meant more to me than playing an obscure tune.

The goal of this era of American fiddling was to see who could play "Sally Goodin," "Tom and Jerry," "Grey Eagle," and "Dusty Miller" the best. Almost all the emphasis was put on these tunes. There were things on the periphery like "Tugboat," but everyone was vying for the best versions of all of them.

17

SP: When I interviewed him a few years ago, Benny said that, as far as teaching you, he thought he had had something to do with "straightening out" your approach to hoedowns. What was he referring to?

MO: I remember him using that word. He was referring to his refinement of the most melodic way to play a tune. When Benny Thomasson plays, you sit there and say, "There cannot be a better rendition!" When he used the term "straighten out," he was straightening out the old fiddle tunes. He made them legitimate musical pieces.

In my attempts at varying and improvising at that time, I would say to him, "I'm getting too far from the melody" or "I wasn't doing something tasteful." He would say, "Let me straighten you out on the bowing, or the emphasis of what I think the tune means and reflects."

SP: How did he teach bowing?

MO: He mainly taught me melody, but I was always watching his bowing. He could slow down some of it. It got across to me that it wasn't exactly the bowing he used because, like mine now, they were always different, except for a few key phrases. It was like, bowing was an attitude and once you got the attitude the bowing is going to be right there. You can go three and one [e.g., ♫♫] or two and two [e.g., ♫♫] or one and three [e.g., ♫♫].

You can get it to sound good.

Mark playing a tune for Benny Thomasson and Frank Hicks at the Weiser Junior High campground, June 1974.

The only way that I learned bowing was by watching. There was no way to get it from records. A perfect case in point is a friend of mine who really is a talented fiddler. The first time he came to Weiser he already was a pretty heavy young classical violinist. He got totally into fiddling and got all the records. The smooth bowing really threw him to where he thought it was all one bow stroke. He'd play, literally maybe 15–20 notes per stroke. He didn't know where the rhythmic aspect came from. He just heard the incredibly smooth-sounding bow. So that's how he played his tunes when he first came to Weiser. Benny Thomasson got a hold of him and straightened him out right away. He was never the same afterwards. It's hard to play as smooth as Benny does going back and forth.

That's an example of why it was so important to be around, looking at somebody doing this incredibly perfect bowing.

The bowing is very rhythmic, but not in patterns. That's what I've always thought. I didn't like fiddling with pattern bowing. My approach is to drive it, really rhythmic with the bow, but never patterns. Never [sings] ♩ ♫ ♩ ♫ for the whole song. You can do that to "Grey Eagle" or "Sally Goodin." [He proceeds to do just that.] That's hard . . . to get it perfectly in time.

Somehow you have to improvise with your bowing and make it turn you on rhythmically. That's what Benny Thomasson did. I've always tried to keep my bow strokes interesting and never get out of time. Never use patterns for more than a couple of bars. Get into that for effect only.

SP: Did Benny start with a simple version or go right into the way he played it?

MO: Right in. I consider his version old-time. His ornamentation is the great way to play. To some people that's a step further. He might have been controversial, but it was hard for me to think of a 65-year-old as controversial.

SP: You were at his place for a couple of days at a time. What did you do besides playing?

MO: Bea [Benny's wife] would always cook a great meal. [Laughs.]

SP: What was her attitude?

MO: She was used to it. She loved the young people being around. She was like grandma to everybody. There were lots of young people taking lessons. Many would impose on him greatly . . . fly cross-country. Word got out that there was this jewel in Washington. Make yourself at home. He had a hard time saying no.

We did some fishing. A lot of times, people would come over at night, or he'd tell stories about the old days. He dug out a tape of him in the late '40s at some contest. I don't know where that tape is now. It is the best fiddling ever possible. Perfect intonation with good tone, and **fast.** It was dazzling.

[. . . people start screaming. It sounds like a football game. He gets up there and plays cross-key "Black Mountain Rag" — you can do anything in Texas — and the announcer, during the tune, was yelling, "Get him off the stage! He's too good!" (Quoted from *Contest Fiddling* by Stacy Phillips)]

SP: Only Texas fiddlers knew about him.

A small part of the Benny Thomasson legacy. Standing: Kevin Bennet, Joe Sites, Jeff Pritchard, Bea Thomasson, Mark O'Connor. Middle: Benny Thomasson. Kneeling: Jeanette Beyer, J'Anna Jacoby, Michelle O'Connor, Loretta Brank, Barbara Lamb. June 1978.

MO: He had chances to become a professional of some magnitude . . . in Gene Autry movies, to sign with a major film company in the '40s, and to play with Bob Wills.

He was a family man and didn't want to leave the house. He felt incredible responsibility to his family. He was so humble with his gift that he could not be talked into it. His worth was good enough for him. He was a Texas fiddler. That's where he was from and that was fine.

[SP: How come you didn't take up the fiddle as a profession?

Benny Thomasson: I had a few kids, and you can't get away. They probably wouldn't have been worth killing now if I'd left. (Laughs.) (Quoted from *Contest Fiddling* by Stacy Phillips.)]

MO: [Robert] "Georgia Slim" Rutland once drove out from Tennessee to see him.

SP: He had somehow heard his name.

MO: He knocked on the door and said, "I'm Georgia Slim Rutland and I've heard that you are the greatest fiddle player in the world. Would you please play for me?" Benny said okay and got out his fiddle. Georgia Slim got on the floor and cried. He couldn't believe it!

SP: What a story!

Who did you learn from besides Benny?

MO: I've got this list of fiddlers, everybody I have physically learned from. [See **"Acknowledgments."**]

SP: Could you fill in some of the other things that led to you becoming a fiddler?

MO: I was 8 years old, studying classical and flamenco guitar. I begged my mom and dad for a fiddle to the point where I tried to make one out of cardboard. It's still intact. I never got around to the stage of putting on strings. By 11 they finally gave in and bought me a $50 fiddle. They couldn't afford much and had put money into my guitar and lessons. But I begged so long they finally got one.

Immediately I took to it and started picking out Doug Kershaw tunes. I got my first lesson a week after, and in three weeks I had learned three tunes, "Boil Them Cabbage Down," "Soldier's Joy," and "Arkansas Traveller." Then I went to a square dance and played all night, the same three tunes. It was more fun that I could have imagined. I started to improvise a little on the tunes. I switched a note here and there and slid into a note. I wanted to avoid monotony. I was easily bored, and boredom gave me the urge to start improvising. After three weeks I was already stretching it, plus I could keep time. Here I was bogged way down in the beginning range of classical guitar after four years. There's no rhythm, and I'm playing slow arpeggios and bar chords. Suddenly I'm grooving [on fiddle] . . . kicking it. There was immediate gratification.

After seven months Weiser came.

SP: The one Barbara Lamb prepared you for.

MO: Yeah. I met a local backup guitar player and entered the Junior-Junior contest and placed second. I had no idea how well I would do. I remember playing "Jolie Blonde" for a waltz, "Florida Blues," and another blues. It was funny because playing the blues was not the thing to do. I was immediately drawn to the sliding sound. That week and the week after were important points in my fiddle education. I was flabbergasted with all the music, taping everything. The week after, I started to apply it. I felt I could do more than I knew. My mind was beyond my physical technique, and I knew how I wanted to play. Somehow I knew the finer points of listening.

SP: Were there any kids your age that you hooked up with?

MO: My outlet was the adult community. At the local contests there were kids my age, one in particular, Loretta Brank. We were Benny Thomasson's favorite students. She won [the Junior-Junior's] that year. She had already been studying with Benny.

There was a bluegrass crowd, but I wanted Texas fiddle so bad . . . and Benny Thomasson was there! When it came time to play at the local mall, I had to teach people Texas-style chord progressions. After a while it became easier to play what they were playing, which was bluegrass. I almost played bluegrass by default.

When you grew up in Seattle, you didn't have the luxury of being [musically] segregated. There were only a few of us. But the Texas fiddle people hated bluegrass, bluegrass people hated Texas fiddle. Eastern old-timers hated Texas fiddle. Cape Breton and French-Canadian fiddlers hated each other. Right away I found that out. There were people that appreciated what I was doing, but they didn't like that style of fiddling . . . or it wouldn't sound right playing with them. That's when I started to adapt. If I was going to play at jam sessions, I'm going to have to play their music. I was 12 and in the learning mode. I played some bluegrass, country, and old-timey.

SP: During the year were you preparing for the next summer's contests?

MO: Through Benny's encouragement. He would turn me loose. I'd rearrange something and play it for him, and he'd say, "That's good, but maybe if you did this and this. . . ." He would improve my arranging skills. First it was giving me the freedom and confidence to mess with it, and then, occasionally, he'd draw me back in.

I remember one time on "Limerock" I thought I had the first part and I was anxious to skip over it and get on to the next section. He said, "Let's back up here. What if you do it with this fingering and phrasing." I'd go, "I'm doing something like this." He'd cause me to really listen to it. I learned from that. I was making my version, but it wasn't even close to being equal to his. It was time for quality control. I realized that there was taste involved. Not really musical taste but common sense . . . going over the obvious. I missed the obvious.

Maybe I played

"Yeah, I got it . . . some trills. Let's do the next part." He goes, "Now, Mark, if you did . . ."

I realized that in among all those trills there's a really pretty melody. My version sounded so blah, straight and unpretty. All flash but no content.

SP: He knew where the melody was coming from and you were one step removed.

MO: Right. I missed the point. He did a lot of that with me.

SP: Could you talk about your relationship with your fiddle elders besides Benny Thomasson, when you started to compete.

MO: They took to me right away. When I was 12 and 13, everybody loved me. It was a combination at being surprised at my age and how long I had been playing. The music I was playing was not in any way bastardizing like I was about to do when I was 14. [Laughter.] At 13, I was also pushing my abilities to the limit, which happened to be where most of my elders were at. At 14 to 16, I started pushing the scope of old-time fiddling. I had the knowledge of the music as far as rhythm, attitude-wise, and bowings. But I started to improvise more in a jazz style and I was in-between for a while. This new, aggressive fiddle style turned on a lot of kids, but it turned off older fiddlers. Many of them complained.

SP: Did you lose some contests because of this?

MO: Oh, yeah. The only ones I didn't lose were at Weiser in the Junior Division when I was 14 and 15. I could lose tons of points and still scrape by winning. I think it was pretty close.

I won the Grand Masters at 13 when I played pretty straight, but then I lost at ages 15, 16, and 17. I thought I was doing the right thing. I was playing better . . . stuff that was complicated and pushing the limit. [When we reviewed some of the transcriptions from this period, Mark was surprised at how difficult some of the music was.] If I played it well I should have scored well.

SP: You obviously had something, because you've spawned a couple of generations of Mark O'Connor clones — little kids who you've got to take some responsibility for. [Laughter.] There are some obnoxious little fiddlers around.

Once you showed it could be done, it was so much easier for the next generation.

MO: Yes. I felt that, even as tasteless as I got, I was in some art form. What I was doing **wasn't** tasteless. I felt I had integrity in whatever I did, whether it was to catch people off guard — people do that with painting, or poetry, or music.

What I tried to do, though I probably abused the privilege, was to make the improvised parts marry the tune.

SP: Some of your variations may become part of the standard renditions for a future generation of fiddlers.

MO: I probably was a little frustrated in that I didn't have the musical outlets I would have liked as a 14-year-old living in Seattle . . . not even able to enter a club until I was 21. There wasn't much to do with my music.

SP: You weren't the first to go far out with a fiddle tune.

MO: Vassar Clements and Scotty Stoneman.

SP: And the guys who played with Bob Wills. You can imagine what some New York City fiddle players used to do to some tunes. You did it under controlled circumstances and, as wild as you got, you were still restraining yourself.

MO: There were some things I would never forfeit . . . rhythm, timing, and drive. I wouldn't go out on a timing limb. I didn't totally leave the things that turned me on about fiddling.

SP: Do you remember the process of working up these new arrangements?

MO: Because I knew all the guitar chords, I remember working out arpeggios to the chordal pattern one time, as an exercise. I put that into "Grey Eagle," I think. I figured out some of my own music theory. I took what I learned one step further, only to learn that it had been done for centuries. [Laughs.] I listened to the harmony and figured out how the passing sounds would relate to the next chord.

SP: Playing around with new chords gave you melodic ideas?

MO: Yeah. [During this time] I didn't play enough. Most of the stuff came pretty fast. I was skateboarding at this time. That's all I did from 14–17. Fiddle on the weekends. In the summer I would play more because I would travel to contests.

SP: So when you were stretching things, your age peers liked it and the older people didn't.

MO: They thought that I was confused and that I should be playing in a jazz combo.

SP: How about Benny?

MO: He liked it all.

SP: He probably faced similar things when he created his approach.

MO: Yeah, he probably related to it.

SP: How much of what you play in this book was improvised on the spot? As opposed to bowing and fingering worked out in advance.

MO: Surprisingly there was more improvisation than you would think. I didn't know exactly what I was going to do. My fingers didn't automatically fall in the same place every time. It was touch and go . . . good luck . . . I don't know what's going to happen.

I had the basic shapes, maybe I would play a whole part the same way. When I started improvising at 13 it might have been a bowing, slide, or safe alternate fingering.

SP: Subtle changes.

MO: When I was 14 I not only worked out new parts, but I improvised.

SP: The most far-out stuff, like the lick in "Sally Johnson"? [See the introduction to that tune in the text.]

MO: That was planned. I had choices to pick from, and I didn't know which one I'd choose. I had played them so many times. I'd begin

There were so many options just in that one lick. Most of them that would make sense to me, I have played by now, though I might come up with a little twist.

Maybe I've never done that [last phrase] before. I call it "controlled improvisation."

Here's another shape.

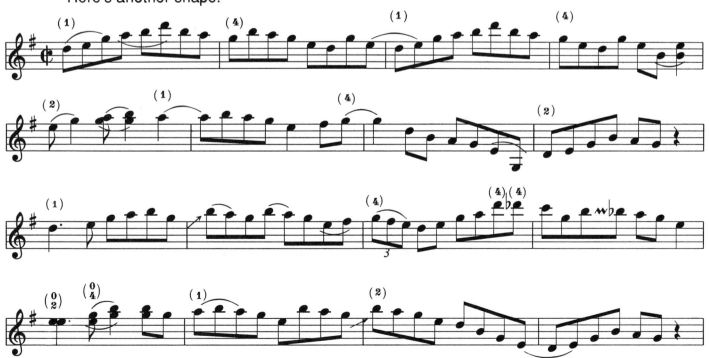

I'm basically in that same shape. So I could

The possibilities are endless. The same with the next shape.

I can go up and down in the same shape . . . controlled improvisation.

SP: You're not on automatic pilot, either. I can see that you're thinking.

MO: Thinking really hard.

SP: Not just finger patterns . . . you're making things melodic and logical.

MO: I can tell when people go into finger patterns, and I hate that sound. That's one of my peeves. When they get to a point where their brain fries and they go into an automatic finger pattern. I'm concentrating so hard on every note to give it value.

SP: It shows. Most of the people who copy you have everything memorized. One of your gifts is being able to think so fast.

MO: Even as we're speaking, my mind is still on that passage and I'm imagining playing. In a sense I'm composing in my head.

I just thought of that.

[Laughs.]

SP: Do you mind if I transcribe some of this for the book?

MO: Sure. I mean I'm kind of tipsy. (Laughs.) [We had just returned from a Mexican meal replete with margaritas.]

SP: All right!

MO: I'm not as focused as I would be on stage . . . really going for it. But starting at 14, you can hear improvising elements. There are many moves that I do that you can hear a lot. [He pointed out a couple of licks in "Sally Johnson" in the text as typical: the last four notes in measure 5, and the first four in measure 5, and measures 41–46.] I did that all the time.

To what extent I improvised all the time . . . I'm not certain. The same tunes I played at contests, I played in jam sessions where I'd be throwing in extra things. When I got to the contest I didn't improvise as much. Maybe I stuck to stuff that I knew I had done before, though not their placement. I remember the feeling of being able to improvise in contests.

Not having it made up . . . people saying, "Aren't you scared you might not know what to do?"

At that point, for one, I didn't care much. I was just going for it. By the time I started to care, I was able to do it fluently. In the later stages like "Sally Ann" [page 176], I didn't have all that worked out. I had the basic shapes.

SP: The spontaneity shows, not mechanical at all.

How about describing the scene at Weiser.

MO: It's a small town [about 5,000 population, which doubles at contest time]. All the local shops have fiddle music playing over their speakers. They paint fiddlers' pictures in each store window . . . cartoons.

The contest lasts a week. People start coming Sunday and leave the next Sunday. The contest is from Monday to Saturday.

SP: How many contestants were there when you competed?

MO: Three hundred and fifty.

SP: Where did you stay?

MO: The townspeople rented spare rooms.

SP: I assume that there was lots of jamming and some people never bothered listening to the contest.

MO: The jamming gave the fiddlers great practice. I really needed it. I didn't practice that much, so when I got to Weiser I got into high gear. This was when I was skateboarding, starting at 14.

SP: You were really serious about skateboarding. I remember that you had a ramp in your back yard.

MO: A half pipe, made out of wood.

SP: What music did you listen to at that time?

MO: Lots of jazz . . . old jazz and the new fusion stuff. About 16 or 17, I started listening to the Top 40.

SP: Getting back to the contest, why did you use two guitarists?

MO: Any discrepancy of one guitar player would be covered.

SP: Didn't they have to practice what they were going to do together?

MO: No. The style lends itself to total chaos. They could hit a bunch of out chords. It's more of a feeling that I was looking for . . . a kick-in-the-butt rhythm. They also played better when they were with someone else. They could try a chord and not be afraid of losing time.

Mark and Joe Sites accompanying Benny Thomasson on a round at Weiser, June 1980.

SP: It's a pretty specialized form of backup. Did you ever accompany other people?

MO: A lot. Early on, that was really a big kick. But later on when I was competing for the Open, starting out at about 17, I had to cut it out.

SP: How did you prepare just before you went on stage?

MO: It was a difficult situation. The warm-up room was madness . . . all kinds of fiddlers going on at the same time . . . very loud. While one fiddler was on stage, the next was escorted to the locker room. It's really echoey, colder and quiet. From there you went out to the stage.

SP: You'd play right up to the moment you competed?

MO: Yeah. Until I heard the applause for the fiddler before me.

The stage is in the center of the gymnasium, and people are seated all around. The microphone comes from the top. It's difficult to play. You can hear a pin drop. You don't hear the sound system. The closest thing to it is playing on the set of a TV show . . . like a hospital, a sterile atmosphere.

[You walk out and they say where you're from, and you get the applause, and you step up there, man it's like a do-or-die thing. So many people lose it . . . because they couldn't handle the pressure. (Quoted from *Contest Fiddling* by Stacy Phillips)]

SP: And it's over real fast.

MO: They put in a timer when I started entering the Open.

[There's a four-minute time limit, so there's no clapping between songs, and that's weird. You've got to go right into the waltz. It's a nerve-wracking experience. (Quoted from *Contest Fiddling*)]

MO: [The time limit] was a big source of controversy.

SP: Who wanted the change?

MO The Chamber of Commerce [who runs the contest].

SP: They put it in because there were so many contestants?

MO: Yeah. It was controversial because a lot of people looked at it as their chance to play. "I came a long way. I don't want to play a breakdown that's a minute long."

SP: Did they talk about cutting down the number of tunes per round?

MO: There was talk of having one elimination round with one tune, but that caused even more controversy. Some people were better waltz players or tune-of-choice.

SP: It would have had to be a hoedown.

MO: The first year I was in the Open, I was 16, the youngest ever to be in the Open. Everybody was real excited. Before that you had to be 18. I had a shot at winning, but I was still playing progressive. In my fifth round on Saturday night with the top eight [finalists] . . . where they cut down to the top five . . . for the waltz I played "Memory Waltz" [a difficult tune from the Howdy Forrester repertoire]. This was the first year of the time limit. None of us had had much experience cutting the tunes so short. Plus the experience of having no applause was weird in itself. I had never got to play on Saturday night, and I was nervous. I had been in the Junior Division, which was wrapped up Wednesday night. This was a big deal for me.

I finished the breakdown and, in order to save time, you go right into the next tune. I jumped into it, and my first three notes were not the ones needed to start this waltz. I tried to recover, but I forgot the melody . . . totally. It freaked me out. I almost put that on the album as a joke, but it was so sick. The tape is pretty darn scary. Everyone was holding their breath. You could feel the tension. You don't want to see anybody lose it. It was simply because I didn't take a breath and concentrate to think how the next tune goes. I could not get back on track. It's almost like I improvised a waltz. I couldn't get back into "Memory Waltz" until about half-way through. But then it would have been obvious that it was a mistake. My mind was fighting. "What to do? What to do?" I pretty much made up a mediocre waltz.

The guitars were all over the place. They were kind of following me. They were hitting wrong chords against each other, and that wasn't helping things. It was sort of a weird version of "Mark's Waltz" off my *Pickin' in the Wind* album. But it was terrible.

30

I might have fooled some of the people, but probably not. I heard comments, "I never heard that waltz before." I was steaming inside, but I didn't say that I blew it because I didn't want to jinx myself. That was the big nightmare.

I placed second.

SP: The judges must have known.

MO: They don't get the titles.

SP: They turn off their speakers and don't get the names of the contestants.

MO: Yes.

SP: Any gamesmanship you can remember where they tried to throw you off your stride?

MO: Well [long pause], it happened to me at other contests. At Weiser, people took it way more seriously. On the contest circuit, there's a lot more of that stuff. At most, there were some psychological games at Weiser . . . no practical jokes. It's such an intense situation.

[Mark later sent me a list, at my request, of a few psych-out ploys used by other contestants when he was a teenager:

1. Tried to get me drunk.
2. Made me try dipping snuff for the first time.
3. Fiddlers would tie up my accompanists so I couldn't practice enough with them.
4. Someone would claim that they heard an inside rumor that the judges were giving me low scores.
5. When I got done playing a round, a fiddler might comment that he had heard mistakes.
6. Some would complain to the officials that I was a professional and should not be allowed to compete.
7. "How can anyone from Seattle know what real fiddling is?"
8. Some would really try to keep me up all night and jam before an early morning round.]

SP: Yet you said you had a good time at jam sessions and stuff. It must have changed when you entered the Open.

MO: My stomach was nervous the whole week. You have six rounds to look forward to. It took forever. You waited for the next cut [announcing survivors into the next round]. Once I was in the jam sessions, it was fun, but it wasn't a relaxed time for me. This was a big goal. [In the Junior-Junior and Junior divisions] Tuesday and Wednesday, and that was it. The rest of the week I hung out and had a good time. Part of it is that people build this up in their mind. It could just be looking at the list of past winners. These are the best.

SP: Some people work towards it the whole year.

MO: Yes, they do. They make it their yearly focus. For me it was almost as if I had grown up there . . . playing in front of your own people. It was such a huge, auspicious fiddling occasion, like a little fiddle heaven.

SP: I'd like to talk a bit about the qualities that differentiate the kind of performances in this book from other American folk fiddling. How about the bowing?

MO: It's usually associated with a real limber wrist. I think that's where the term "long bow" came in.

SP: But you do a lot of single strokes.

MO: It isn't necessarily long, but it looks long because of the wrist action. [He proceeds to play two versions of a fiddle tune. Using a limber wrist, there is almost no discernible space between the notes, even though there is mostly one note per bow stroke. Without the "Texas wrist," a space between the notes becomes a bit noticeable.] All of a sudden it's something else, Canadian maybe.

SP: Contest style really has smooth bow changes. It also seems that triplets are more prevalent than in other Southern styles.

MO: In Ireland there are triplets all over the place. In Appalachia they lost that technique.

SP: Well, I'm not sure that Texas fiddling in the 1920s had triplets . . . Eck Robertson? It might have been something that came in the Benny Thomasson era. I don't know.

MO: You're right that Eck Robertson didn't have a lot of triplets. As the fiddling became more technically dazzling, maybe.

SP: How about the backup?

MO: It makes me play differently. The melody may be good no matter what you have behind it. There's no doubt I change my groove with bluegrass or Texas chords behind "Sally Goodin." I can't tell you what I do. From an early age I tried to be adaptive to whomever I played with. There's a different feel to Texas style. It's a little magic.

SP: It seems that the fourth note of the scale is often sharped, like C♯ in the key of G, and F♯ in C.

MO: [Plays a bit.] And G♯ in D. [Plays some more.] It's not as common in A. It might have something to do with the basic hand positions in those keys. That's probably why the F♯ is often used in C position, because it doesn't feel the greatest to drop the first finger down [to play F on the E string]. It's like an idiosyncrasy of fiddling.

If it works in C it should work in A, but it actually sounds more foreign to my ears hearing it in A. I feel like I'm in another country. It feels awkward.

SP: It may just be the way you're trained to play in A as opposed to C. A has all that open-string and drone stuff, and C has a whole different approach.

MO: Yeah.

SP: What would "Billy in the Lowground" sound like in A? You probably wouldn't use the sharped fourth note.

MO: No. [Plays that tune in A.] I'm playing D natural. One of the neat things on fiddle is the way tunes lend themselves to certain keys . . . using open strings as much as you can.

SP: Benny Thomasson loosened the ties between certain tunes and keys, like playing in third position in the key of C opens a new set of possibilities.

What are some of the typical misconceptions of fiddlers who are just learning the contest style?

MO: It can happen with any type of traditional music, but it's nothing to be ashamed of. Some blatant misunderstanding, like improvising to where it leaves the shape of the tune.

SP: If you're not well grounded in the music, a learner might take something wild that you just tried, to be an integral part of the tune, and work from there. They begin to lose touch.

MO: [Laughs.] Yeah. Probably, to many people's ears I was leaving the tune. To my mind it still sounded like that tune. You could snip out a whole section and still know what tune I was playing.

SP: I can imagine some time in the future, you hearing someone in a contest and saying, "You're real good but maybe you should come back a bit to the melody," and that fiddler shaking his head like, "You old fogey!"

MO: In the later years [represented in this book] I'm still varying "Arkansas Traveller" and "Herman's Hornpipe," but closer. That was to answer those who said, "Mark is hot but he can't play the tune." I'm playing just fancy enough to impress the people who want to hear the technique, but enough of the tune to impress the old-time purist. I was going for the taste contest. I wanted to set a new standard for old-time fiddle playing.

SP: For clarity?

MO: And tone and pitch.

Interpreting the Transcriptions

Mark and I have striven for accuracy in these transcriptions, which makes for occasional densely notated passages. However, all the included information will enable you to play the music authentically, as Mark envisioned it. Using this book in conjunction with the companion album should dispel most difficulties.

Veteran sight readers will have no particular problems with this music. However, for the goodly percentage of this book's audience that learns by ear, omitting some of the embellishments when first working up a tune can simplify the process. Initially, leave out the grace notes and slides, and play everything with single bow strokes. Play only the first notes of any triplets, and sustain that note for the duration of the entire triplet (i.e., quarter or eighth note). When you can play this stripped-down version of a passage, begin to reintroduce the ornaments and bowings.

Mark makes many short, sometimes almost imperceptible slides on up-tempo tunes. Even the most obscure of them add a bit of zest to his playing.

MO: For example, in "Billy in the Lowground" I'm not going

I'm going

The slides are so quick. I may sound like I'm hitting the note [squarely], but I'm moving my hand back and forth all the time, aggressively.

In all my fiddle books, I have raved on about the correct phrasing of eighth notes. I know it is having some small effect, because I have finally begun to notice similar warnings recently by other authors. You should be aware that a series of eighth notes should not be phrased exactly as written. The first note of each pair of eighths should be slightly longer than the second. At the tempo of these tunes, the phrasing should be somewhere **between** even; i.e., literally

and tied triplets

(i.e., a heavy swing feel). This subtlety is sometimes notated as

(i.e., slightly legato followed by slightly staccato). The waltzes have the most pronounced tied-triplet character of the tunes in this book. Be aware that the exact eighth-note relationship is not static, and slight variations add a jaunty looseness to the rhythm.

The bowings have been carefully notated, but it is virtually impossible to get them 100% accurate. If a particular passage seems awkward, add or subtract a slur. Playing the same piece at different tempos may also suggest different bowings.

Here are some music symbols with which you may not be familiar, including some non-standard notation that I find useful for fiddle music:

1) The numbers in parentheses above the staff tell you which finger to use.

2) A "degree" symbol (°) above a note means to play that note as a natural harmonic.

3) Drones are notated separately, so

means to sustain an A note with your pinky while playing the four indicated eighth notes.

4) ⋁ means "play with an up bow." ⊓ means "play with a down bow."

5) ⨎ indicates a "fake" bowing of all the strings simultaneously, utilizing a fast down bow stroke, starting on the G string. (See "Allentown Polka," measure 51.)

6) There are three variants of slide notation:

a)

means to hold the A♯ for its assigned duration, then quickly slide to B. **Do not change fingering or bow direction.**

b)

means to begin a slide immediately upon fingering the F♯. The F♯ has no duration.

c)

means a quick flick of a slide, usually a half step or less in length.

7) When a note appears in parentheses **with** rhythmic notation (as opposed to 6b on the previous page) it indicates a ghost note, a note that seems to be there but is either covered up by the accompaniment or "swallowed" in the welter of notes that surround it.

8) The Roman numerals demarcate the beginning of new sections. These are Mark's perceptions of different parts or variations of the tunes.

1975

This was the second year that Mark competed in, and won, the Junior Division at Weiser. He classifies these renditions as part of the first phase of his playing style. At 13 years of age, his execution is exceptional.

MO: The first phase started in 1975. . . . At this point, I was already playing with a distinct personal style, developing my own arrangements of tunes, and playing them as clean as I could. [Quoted from the notes of the album of the music contained in this book]

Mark was just beginning to realize his gifts as a fiddler, and the fiddle world began to hear tales of a new prodigy.

Benny Thomasson's influence is particularly evident in 1975.

The five finalists in the Junior Division, June 1975. Left to right: Ken Smith, Ron Wolbauer, Jeff Pritchard, Loretta Brank, and Mark.

Grey Eagle 1

"Grey Eagle" is one of the core hoedowns of the Texas-style contest repertoire, and many of this style's and Mark's characteristics are apparent in this transcription. Among the traits of this manner of playing are:

a) liberal use of the third hand position (e.g., measure 57 and on),

b) hemiolas, i.e., repeated three-note patterns, giving rise to syncopation (measures 7–8),

c) frequent quarter- and eighth-note slurred triplets,

d) bow rocking and generally strategically placed string changing for rhythmic drive (e.g., measures 4–5 and 23),

e) a fingered A (or E) followed by the same note on an open string (e.g., measure 36),

f) flat 3rds and sharp 4ths as passing tones (here C natural or B$\sharp$, and D$\sharp$),

g) mostly one note per bow stroke, with more slurs in upper positions.

Mark quotes from "Limerock" in measures 93–94 and uses one of Benny Thomasson's favorite licks in measures 21–22.

All the parts can be accompanied by the same chord progression, though Section IV is the only one with an obvious | A | D | A | E | sequence. Mark played this at a metronome setting of 109.

¢	‖ A A9/C$\sharp$	D D$\sharp$°	A A/C$\sharp$ A/C$\natural$	E7/B E7/G$\sharp$ ‖
		A A9/C$\sharp$	D D$\sharp$°	E7 E7/G$\sharp$	E7 A ‖

Grey Eagle 1

Grandfather Polka 1

This is the older name for "Clarinet Polka," a tune with ultimate roots in Poland. As is typical of contest polkas, each section is in a different key.

The bow rock in measure 34 is an explicit example of Mark's use of bowing for drive. This version is played at MM = 111.

Grandfather Polka 1

Dusty Miller

"Dusty Miller" is a flower and a quilt pattern in addition to being the title of another Texas contest standard. The ♭7 notes (here G♮) give the tune a modal flavor (a mix of major and minor tonality) which is leavened by the strongly major chord accompaniment. In the Southeast, C♯ and C♮ notes are mixed in, and the backup often includes G major chords (as in our measures 35 and 39). This accentuates the modal feel. (It sounds like one of the guitarists occasionally plays a G chord.)

Measures 13 and 61 contain a typical Benny Thomasson two-octave smear of notes that he uses as a signature melodic embellishment. The bow rocking in measures 81 and 93 should again be thought of as rhythmic ornamentations.

The difficult bow pattern in measure 89 is another Thomasson favorite. It will turn up in several other A hoedowns.

Mark played this at MM = 110.

In the fifth measure of sections II and IV, the A chord is played an octave higher. For guitarists, that would involve using an F chord shape around the 7th fret.

I & III	¢ ‖ A A9/C♯	D D♯°	A F♯m	E7 E7/G♯ ‖
	A A9/C♯	D D♯°	E7 E7/G♯	E7 A ‖
II & IV	A A9/C♯	A A9/C♯	E7 E7/G♯	E7/B A
	A C♯m/G♯	F♯m A/C♯	E E/C♯	E7 A ‖

46

Dusty Miller

49

I Don't Love Nobody 1

"I Don't Love Nobody" entered the fiddle world in the key of C, but in the contest circuit an A version evolved. In the process a section in the relative minor key was dropped.

Mark remembers that he meant to play a B at the end of measure 5 and a C at the beginning of measure 6, so invert those two notes.

I recognize a version of a Benny Martin riff in measures 73–74.

Mark played this at MM = 112.

¢ ‖ A A/C♯	A A/C♯	D D/F♯	A A/C♯	
A A/C♯	A A/C♯	B7	E7	
A A/C♯	A A/C♯	D D/F♯	A A/C♯	
D D♯°/F♯	A F♯7	B7 E7	A ‖	

I Don't Love Nobody 1

Wednesday Night Waltz

"Wednesday Night" is filled with the usual contest-style waltz frills — a skittering melodic line and demanding double-stops, all of which Mark handles with unnatural aplomb for a mere stripling.

The beginnings were cut off in the original recordings of "Wednesday Night" and "Sally Goodwin 1"; but, since they were among Mark's favorites, he just chose a convenient entrance point. As a result, this version begins at the second section. The tempo is MM = 131.

The only difference in the chord sequence in the two parts is in measures 23 and 24, where a D is played in Section I and an F$\sharp$7 in Section II.

$\frac{3}{4}$ ‖ D	C$\sharp$7	Bm	D	G	Em	D	A7
D	C$\sharp$7	Bm	D	E	E/G$\sharp$	A7	A7/C$\sharp$
D	C$\sharp$7	Bm	D	G	G	**I** D / **II** F$\sharp$7	D F$\sharp$7
G	G$\sharp$°	D	B7	E7	A7	D	D ‖

54

June 1974, the year of the double winners. Mark won the Junior-Junior and Junior divisions, and Benny won the Open and Seniors.

Wednesday Night Waltz

Herman's Rag 1

"Herman's Rag" is a tune built around one lick and is named for Herman Johnson, another Weiser champion. Note the different bowings for the hemiolas in the melody statements and the wacky run in measure 15. The riff in the 65th measure is borrowed from "Grey Eagle."

Mark played this at MM = 110.

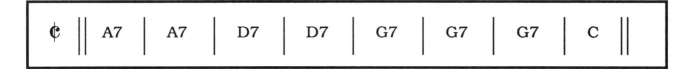

Herman's Rag 1

Sally Goodwin 1

"Sally Goodwin" (or, as I prefer, "Goodin") is the standard by which Texas-style contest fiddlers are measured. There are plenty of opportunities for drones, slides, and searing high-position passages.

The phrasing in measures 21 and 25 was used by both Benny Thomasson and Major Franklin. The latter was an important (and feisty) contemporary of Benny. A couple of sections are omitted in this version, but they can be found in "Sally Goodwin 2."

The tempo is MM = 111. The chording is the same as "Grey Eagle" except for Section VII.

Sally Goodwin 1

1976

This year marks the beginning of Mark's rambunctious period, reflecting a teenager's unabashed probing of any imposed limits.

MO: It was more progressive, wild, and fun to listen to. It contained lots of improvisation, showing more of a jazz-flavored approach to the music. [Quoted from the liner notes for the album of the music in this book]

Look for increased tempos, extended periods of daring upper-position work, more frequent bow-rocking rhythmic thrusts, and flights of bluesy, chromatic fancies. All this is realized with flawless technique and singing tone.

The five finalists in the Junior Division, June 1976. Left to right: Mark, Loretta Brank, Terry Field, Jeff Gurnsey, and Jess Cooper.

Sally Johnson

"Sally Johnson" is **the** standard contest G tune.

MO: [It] was renamed from "Katy Hill." Someone in Texas, Benny Thomasson or one of his cronies, made it into more of a spectacular tune that you'd want to play in a contest. They changed it to an extent that they renamed it.

A prime example of Mark's sassiness is the disturbing run in measures 14–15. It begins as a diminished arpeggio and ends as a finger-pattern lick on the D and G strings.

SP: Okay, O'Connor, come clean. Why'd you do it? [Laughter.]

MO: I'm trying to remember back when I was 14. I think it came from Terry Morris at a jam session that I had taped a year earlier. He was kind of stretching it. It might have been a mistake or something he didn't plan to do. But it sounded so fun that it caught me. So I ended up with something like that mistake and tried to catch people's attention. They would hear it and say, "What just happened?" [Laughter.]

SP: The speakers probably jumped off the wall in the judges' room. [Laughter.] Did you win that year?

MO: Yeah. That was in the Junior Division, so I wasn't up against the real stiff competition of the Open. I could stretch it and get docked a lot [of points] and still come out ahead . . . maybe barely scraping by to win.

The rhythm notation in measures 7 and 111 can only approximate the smear of notes that Mark plays. He stays in third position from measure 44 through 80.

SP: Where Benny might play two consecutive sections in third position, you'd do three or four.

MO: I made up some variations up there.

SP: There are passages that you could play in first position, but you stayed up there.

MO: Now I probably would come down, because I think I can get better tone. I did that for a couple of reasons. It stretched my limits as a player, and I probably felt more comfortable not shifting. I thought shifting often was harder than shifting once and leaving your hand in place for a while.

Back then I didn't have a shoulder rest, so shifting was a lot harder than it is for me now. For many years I held the fiddle up with my hand. I couldn't count on my neck to hold it. I didn't have proper posture. I still have bad habits left over from then.

Note the sudden bow rocking in such measures as 11, 18, and 64. This is one way Mark injects a rhythmic jolt to a phrase. Measure 77 contains a reworking of a classic Johnny Gimble lick from his fiddle hit "Fiddlin' Around." (This is probably the last fiddle single to get commercial airplay.)

Mark played this at MM = 119.

I & V

$\mathbb{C}$ ‖ G G/C♯ | C C♯° | G G/C♯ | B7♯9/F♯ (D/F♯) Em |

| G G/B | C C♯° | D Bm | D/A G ‖

II, III, IV, & VI

‖ G G/B | C C♯° | G G/B | B♭° D7/A |

| G G/B | C C♯° | D Bm | D/A G ‖

Sally Johnson

70

Yellow Rose Waltz

This transcription is difficult to read because of the density of ornamentation. To ease getting started, ignore the grace notes and play the first note of any triplet for the entire duration of the figure, i.e., either an eighth or quarter note. The given timing for beats divided into four or five notes is often approximated, so feel free to reinterpret them.

Check out the tricky fourth-position double-stop harmonic in measures 17 and 18. There are many slithery, nay, even greasy arrays of double-stops of which my favorites are in measures 43–44 and 77–78.

Mark's waltz tempo is down to MM = 123.

I

$\frac{3}{4}$ ‖ F | Am | Dm | F | F | F$\sharp$° | C | C |

(F$\sharp$+) (B♭/F♮)

| Gm | Gm/F$\sharp$ | Gm/F♮ | C | C | C+ | F | F ‖

II

‖ F | Am | Dm | F | F | F7 | B♭ | Gm |

| B♭ | B° | F | D7 | G7 | C7 | F | F ‖

Yellow Rose Waltz

Tom and Jerry 1

"Tom and Jerry" is obviously from the same bag as "Grey Eagle" and "Sally Goodin." Obey the bowings in measures 17–18 to get the correct feel. Measures 49–64 are filled with some of my favorite free-spirited musical moments. Go, Mark!

The tempo is MM = 118

I, III, V, VI, & VII

¢ ‖ A A/C♯ | F♯m F♯m/C♯ | A F♯m | E E/G♯ |

| A A/C♯ | D D♯° | E E/C♯ | E/B A ‖

II & IV

‖ A A/C♯ | D D♯° | E E/C♯ | E/B E/G♯ |

| A A/C♯ | D D♯° | E E/C♯ | E/B A ‖

In measure 110 the " ♯ " notation is a half sharp, midway between F♯ and F♮.

Tom and Jerry 1

1977

At 15 years of age, this was Mark's final win in the Junior Division. Until 1978 there was no four-minute time limit, so this is the last year of relatively long renditions.

The first four-time consecutive winner in the Junior Division at Weiser.

Billy in the Lowground

Mark stays in third position from measures 49 through 88. He is really thumbing his nose at the fiddle conservatives with that final double-stop.

The tempo is MM = 119.

¢ ‖ C	C	Am	Am
C	C	Am G	G/B C ‖

The " 𝄳 " notation in measure 34 is a half flat symbol. Play the note between B♮ and B♭.

Billy in the Lowground

84

85

Herman's Rag 2

Compare this version with "Herman's Rag 1." Here the melody statements have more passing tones, bow rocking, and general busy-ness. The versions are the same length, but there is less repetition here.

Enjoy the chromaticisms beginning at measure 33. The phrasing in measures 35 and 43 indicate that Mark had been listening to swing music. There is some fast hand shifting beginning at measure 49 to allow playing the whole passage on the A string. Mark says that he was attracted by the visual aspect of this maneuver.

The tempo is MM = 118.

Herman's Rag 2

1978

Because of his dominance of the Junior Division, Mark was allowed to compete in the Open category at 16 instead of the previously mandated 18. Conservative judging, progressive playing, and stiffer competition resulted in a second-place finish, but Mark thinks that he did some of his best playing in 1978.

This was the first year of the four-minute-per-round rule, resulting in shorter renditions with some sections omitted and, generally, less room to stretch out.

Left to right: Mark, Herman Johnson, and Junior Daugherty. June 1978.

Allentown Polka

Play this at MM = 117. The accompaniment to Section II is the same as Section I but transposed up a major second interval.

I 𝄵 ‖	G Am	B♭° G/B	G	D	
	D Em	F° D/F♯	D	G	
	G Am	B♭° G/B	G G7	C	
	C C♯°	G E7	A7 D7	G	
	C C♯°	G E7	A7 D7	G ‖

II ‖	A Bm	C° A/C♯	A	E	
	E F♯m	G° E/G♯	E	A	
	A Bm	C° A/C♯	A A7	D	
	D D♯°	A F♯7	B7 E7	A	
	D D♯°	A F♯7	B7 E7	A ‖

Allentown Polka

Mark accompanying Benny Thomasson at the Washington State Fiddlers' Contest, July 1978.

Brilliancy 1

"Brilliancy" comes from a medley of the same name, recorded by Eck Robertson in the 1920s. Mark played this at MM = 111.

As in "Dusty Miller," the first A chord in measure 1 of Section II is played an octave up.

I

¢ ‖ A A/C♯ | F♯m | A F♯m | E E/G♯ |

| A A9/C♯ | D D♯° | E F♯m | E E/G♯ |

II

‖ A C♯m/G♯ | F♯m A/C♯ | D A/C♯ | Bm E |

| A A9/C♯ | D D♯° | E F♯m | E/G♯ A ‖

III

‖ A A/C♯ | A/F♯ A/E | E E/G♯ | E/C♯ E/B |

| A A9/C♯ | D D♯° | E F♯m | E/G♯ A ‖

95

Brilliancy 1

Black and White Rag 1

If Mark had been laying back on the previous two selections, he certainly goes full-tilt "controlled improvisation" in "Black and White Rag." Among the highlights are a) the wild measures 20–24 and 26–27 (measures 23–24 contain the kind of guitar chord-oriented lick that Mark refers to in the interview), and b) the whole last section, climaxing with the frenzy of the final four measures.

There is a third part to this tune which Mark omits. The tempo is MM = 116. The symbols in measures 7–8 of Section I in the chord progression mean to stop the rhythm for two measures.

See "Billy in the Lowground" for an explanation of notation in measure 31.

I $\mathbf{C}$ ‖ D Em | F° D/F♯ | G Am | B♭° G/B |

| D D/F♯ | D D/F♯ | " G | - ‖ " |

| D Em | F° D/F♯ | G Am | B♭° G/B |

| E7 E/G♯ | A A/C♯ | D7 D/F♯ | G ‖

II ‖ C | A7 A/C♯ | D D/F♯ | D D/F♯ |

| G Am | B♭° G/B | C A7 | D7 G7 |

| C | A7 A/C♯ | D D/F♯ | D D/F♯ |

| G Am | B♭° G/B | G G/B | C ‖

John Francis, Dick Barrett, and Mark during the awards ceremony, June 1978.

Black and White Rag 1

Tom and Jerry 2

In the 44th measure of this version of "Tom and Jerry," Mark remembers playing the second D note as a sharp, though I hear it natural. I do agree that a D♯ is sexier. Before the final chord, he slides up to a high A harmonic on the A string.

Amazingly, the tempo is exactly the same as in 1976, MM = 118. Not so amazing is the fact that the chords are also unchanged.

Tom and Jerry 2

Grandfather Polka 2

In this second arrangement of "Grandfather Polka," there are many more chromatic touches and short intervals of bow rocking. The latter result in angular, wide intervallic melodic lines. (See measures 4, 21, 30, and 45–46.)

When I stopped transcribing some of this music and just listened to it, it's really amazing. Like the emcee says at the end of this piece, "Sounds good!"

Mark plays this at MM = 114.

Grandfather Polka 2

Dill Pickle Rag 1

Rags seem to bring out the spunk in Mr. O'Connor. This version of "Dill Pickles" is full of fun stuff that might annoy an old-time music purist but that electrifies free spirits. Measures 23–24 are another example of arpeggiated outlining of guitar chords. In the 30th measure a whole-tone scale whips by. What a wise guy!

It is obvious from the last few measures that Mark is cutting this tune short to conform to the time limits. The tempo is MM = 120.

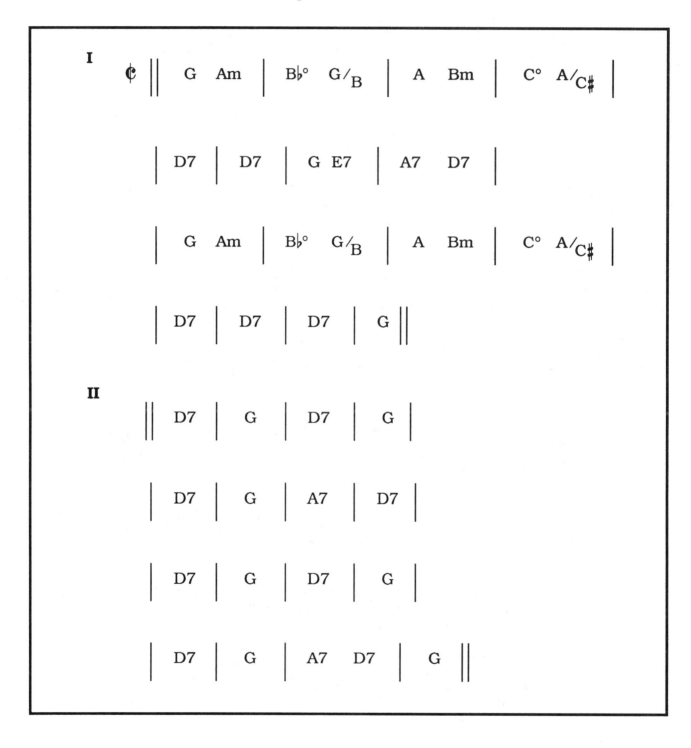

Dill Pickle Rag 1

Interview with Michelle O'Connor

Michelle O'Connor travelled the contest circuit with her brother for about ten years and has a unique viewpoint of those experiences.

Stacy Phillips: Firstly, I'm not going to refer to you as Mark O'Connor's sister.

Michelle O'Connor: That's the way everyone has always referred to me [laughs], Mark's little sister.

SP: You were a contestant for a while.

MiO: I started in the Junior-Juniors and got third two years in a row. I quit when I started ballet at 13.

SP: But you continued to go after that?

MiO: Yes. My last year was '83, I think. It was kind of a way of life. We took off every summer and travelled around in the van.

SP: Your mom, you, and Mark?

MiO: Right. Sometimes Dad would go with us to Nashville and fly back to go to work.

Most of the memories I have of travelling are the best memories. I remember Mom driving all night and Mark and I waking up asking what state we were in. Mom was a pretty incredible person . . . even when she was sick, we didn't know to what extent. I didn't find out she had cancer until I was 16, but she had had it since I was 6.

So I remember her trying to get us to the next contest. We took one trek across country in November, from Philadelphia to Seattle, through snow and sleet, pulling a U-Haul trailer. Mark had played some sort of bluegrass show with Tut Taylor [a Dobro player]. We had gone to Winfield [Kansas contest] in September and then Nashville because we thought we might move there. We rented an apartment for a couple of months. Things didn't work out. We called the apartment "Bugsville." [Laughs.] Mom drove 3,000 miles in the snow and never learned how to back up the trailer. [Laughter.]

SP: What age span were you in this period?

MiO: Mark's first year at Weiser, when he got second in the Junior-Juniors, I was 7. That year I wasn't into it at all. Mom really worried about me. There's a big side of Weiser that's hippie. There are the fiddlers that get into jam sessions, but the rest of it's a hippie festival in campgrounds all over town. But they're separate from the contest.

SP: They're hanging out because there's a scene going on.

MiO: Yeah. That year I wasn't interested in music yet, but the next year I was because I started playing.

SP: Was there a realization in your family early on that Mark really had something?

MiO: Yes. I was too young then to really understand what that meant. Mom was probably the best "show parent" you could ever hope to have. Later on I saw other kids up-and-coming at Weiser, and I could see how their parents treated them . . . [intensely] "You've got this in the bag. You're gonna win this one!" . . . all this "Go, go, go!" . . . like they're at a soccer game.

Mom was totally the opposite. I remember her calmly sitting Mark down. "Well, if you play a **really** good round, you might make the top five, but there are a lot of good players here this year" . . . kind of a pep talk, but always making sure that he never thought he was the best. She never sat anywhere near he could see her at any contest or concert. She never clapped for him. Dad was just the opposite, "Bravo!" . . . the loudest in the audience.

Mom pushed Mark in other ways. She got him to those festivals. She handled his contest money. She saved it for him. He couldn't just take the money and pocket it.

SP: I assume you were inspired to play by Mark.

MiO: My trials and tribulations of playing fiddle [laughs] . . . I had a fair degree of talent. I went home from Weiser every year all enthusiastic, saying I was going to practice every day, and that lasted for a couple of weeks. Then, two weeks before Weiser the next year, I got out the fiddle. Then I'd get mad because I never really improved that much. It wasn't in my blood as much as it was in Mark's. It was a big part of my life but, when I started dancing, I quit. [Michelle is now a professional dancer.]

I remember the year when I was trying to pick things up, but I'd get frustrated because at the contests Mark got the credit for my playing. People would come up and say, "Oh, you're so lucky! You have an older brother like Mark O'Connor to teach you how to play," and on and on. I would throw crying fits, because Mark wouldn't show me anything. There was an age difference there where I was always someone he teased. We had a 16 [rpm] speed on our phonograph. I'd put on fiddle albums, slow them down and tape them onto a cassette, and learned them note for note, an octave lower.

SP: Which albums?

MiO: Usually not Mark's because his were too complicated. I might have learned some stuff off of his first album. I remember Dale Morris, Benny Thomasson, Terry Morris, and "Summertime" off of Texas Shorty's [Jim Chancellor] album.

SP: When Mark first started, did he practice a lot at home?

MiO: Yeah, but when he got into the skateboarding scene in high school, I don't know how he ever wrote "On the Rampage." It didn't seem that he did much but skate that year. He went through different stages. Right before he wrote that, that whole year he was into Jean-Luc Ponty and Joe Venuti.

The most I remember Mark doing around the house was guitar, and I think to this day he still writes a lot of his music on guitar. When he sat down to play the fiddle, he never played tunes. He "dinged" around. He would sit and improvise, and melodies would come out, and that's how he'd end up writing music. It's not as if he sat down and said, "Now I'm going to play "'Sally Goodin.'" I don't remember him ever practicing contest music until right before Weiser came around and Mom would say, "You'd better get your rounds together." You have to set up so many rounds for so many minutes. But he didn't practice contest tunes all year.

My mother taught him his very first fiddle tune, "Louisiana Man" [a Doug Kershaw song]. She was fairly musical though she didn't have the opportunity to develop it. She got the fiddle and picked out the melody off the record and taught it to Mark.

SP: I met your mom once, this was when she was quite ill, but she was working hard for Mark . . . on the phone all the time.

MiO: She took care of everything. There wasn't any Texas fiddle scene in Seattle, but there were bluegrass cliques. It was kind of weird. For a while people in town tried to outcast us from the scene. I heard people say things about Mom . . . how she was pushy and Mark had a big head. They were trying to make something happen.

Mom certainly believed in us, and we knew it and we had confidence. But she wasn't what you would call a pushy stage mother.

SP: It sounds like Mark was recognized more outside Seattle. Still, he must have been some sort of local hero.

MiO: There was a short period of time where we felt like we were being avoided, but it came around after that. When he came back to town he would look everyone up. I was kind of young and didn't know exactly what was going on, but I knew when people would stop coming over. People used to jam at our house all the time. The living room was full and

The Tennesseans with Hank English on guitar and Harley Worthington on banjo.

110

there were instruments all over the floor. Mom always made fried chicken and everyone came to dinner. [Laughs.]

That's when he had the band, The Tennesseans. I played mandolin. We had guitar and banjo . . . Hank and Harley.

SP: Bluegrass?

MiO: Yes. We'd play Dan and Joe's Tavern every other weekend. I used to sing "Rocky Top," my solo. [Laughs.]

SP: Do you still play?

MiO: No. I'm only dancing now.

SP: How many trips did you make per summer?

MiO: A lot of times we would take off and never come back all summer. We would stay at the Days Inn in Nashville, which had a kitchenette, and settle in. Weiser was the first of the season, then Ogden, Utah. Then there was the Crockett, Texas, contest in June, too.

SP: These are long hauls between contests.

MiO: We would usually sleep in the van. We knew people along the way sometimes. In Oklahoma we'd stop at Herman Johnson's, in Kansas at Jeff Pritchard's, and in Dallas we'd stop at the Jerry Thomassons' [Benny Thomasson's son]. If Dad was with us we'd get a hotel and he'd sleep in the van because he snored so loud that we couldn't sleep. [Laughter.] [Otherwise] Mom and I were in the back and Mark slept across the two front seats. Mom had a buffet fetish, so every town we went into we'd stop at a gas station to find a buffet in town. We had to have our vegetables. She never let us have french fries or soda pop.

SP: Did you take lessons from Benny Thomasson?

MiO: Maybe I did take a few. Mark bought that white fiddle from him that he got autographed.

Some people tried to take advantage of Benny. He was the sweetest, dearest man I could ever hope to meet. There wasn't a person out there who didn't love him to death. Bea [Benny's wife] would begin to get irritated, but she didn't mind when we came around. Mark was genuine. There were formal lessons. We paid.

I might have taken a lesson or two from him. I took a few from John Burke, who is someone that Mark took from a little bit. I used to accompany him to his lessons and wait for him. It was a big part of my life. I really miss it sometimes. I find myself dating musicians. Music is such a part of me that I want it back in my life again.

SP: Speaking as a musician, I would recommend that you avoid them. [Laughter.]

MiO: Did Mark tell you about the cardboard fiddles?

SP: He said he started to build one.

MiO: Right, and I did everything he did, so I built one, too.

111

David Johns accompanying Mark in 1976. Mark collected autographs of great fiddlers on the white violin and later donated it to the Country Music Hall of Fame.

Mom also used to put on shows at the theater in Shoreline College. She did one with Byron Berline and Sam Bush and one with Charley Collins and Oswald Kirby. She did another with Josh Graves. It took a lot of work. She promoted them and did the printing and ads on the radio.

Those were memorable times. The performers knew we didn't have a lot of money and we would be happy to break even. So they would stay at our house instead of a hotel. The whole upstairs of our house was a ballroom. Our parents met while ballroom dancing. They were both teachers at Arthur Murray [Dance Studios]. Dad did the construction. It was sort of like *The Waltons* [TV show], everyone in one room.

Mark and I always fought at home; but, as soon as he moved out and went with the [David Grisman] Quintet when he turned 18, we started getting real close. He took me on his tours of Japan and the Middle East.

SP: One thing I found interesting was his experience at school in his teen years. He says it was rough for him. Do you remember that?

MiO: I followed in his footsteps. When I tried to get into the high school singing group, the guy who directed it was the person who had him for independent study in Mark's senior year. The teacher hated doing that.

And the kids called him "Fiddle Faddle from the Fiddle Farm" and "Brace Face Tin Teeth" because he got braces when he was 12. In elementary school, when he was playing classical [guitar] he'd play for special events, but when the kids got old enough to make fun of something different, he really clammed up about it.

He used to sing Johnny Cash tunes before his voice changed. He had a really high voice. He wouldn't sing after that.

I remember when he finally did the independent study, it was with electric guitar, bass, and drums. He wrote and arranged all the music for the trio. They met three hours a day out back behind the shop. That was when the kids at school started to accept him because they heard him playing electric music.

At the final school music showcase, which is what they had worked towards for the performance of their numbers, the director came out to introduce the band in a very derogatory tone . . . talking about selling ear plugs. But all the kids loved it. Came graduation time, at the ceremony, there were so many awards called out for the school band and choir. Mark wasn't recognized for anything. Not only did he not win anything, but he wasn't even recognized.

SP: The guy was world renowned by then.

MiO: Mom was crying. She felt bad about his experience at school.

SP: Was she aware of what was going on?

MiO: Oh, yeah, but sometimes parents don't understand the full extent of what their kids go through. But at that moment she realized how hard school had been for him. Mark and Mom talked a little bit, then Mark said, "I gotta go pack," and the next day he flew to Nashville to enter the Grand Masters. His life was moving on.

I found this letter when we were looking through Mom's stuff, to the school superintendent, about him being unrecognized. She didn't send it. We had a bad high school.

SP: He said that one reason he skateboarded was . . .

MiO: . . . to be accepted. It helped him. [Our parents] let him rip up our back yard and build the half pipe. That's why they let him do things like that. Number one, it would keep the kids in the neighborhood at our house. Mom didn't want him going off and getting in trouble. O'Connor's was the place to hang out. It gave him some prestige. He was excellent at it. He could have been a professional. He had a lot of talents.

Mom had a lot of talent, but her parents didn't give her the opportunity. She got sick when we were so young. I think she lived her life through us in a lot of ways. If there was one piece of advice that came from Mom it was, "Always keep an open mind." She raised us to be independent and to take care of ourselves.

SP: Getting back to Weiser, what did you do after your competition?

MiO: We were always hanging around where the fiddlers hung out and jammed. That was the best part of Weiser. No one hardly went in to watch the contest. That was the most boring thing to do.

SP: Until the final round.

MiO: Right. Wherever Jerry Thomasson was, was where the jam session would start.

SP: Because he was the best rhythm player?

MiO: Yes. He played tenor guitar and was the most in demand. I remember watching Dick Barrett and Benny Thomasson. Dale Morris quit coming after the first few years, Junior Daugherty was there, and Jeff Pritchard. We hung out with the people from Texas. The bluegrassers were in a different section. But everyone knew the O'Connor van.

SP: What about the Texas contests? How was Crockett different from Weiser?

MiO: In Texas the person that lost took the winner's trophy and stomped it in the mud! [Laughter.]

[A reliable source says that there was no real stomping, just a joke among friendly rivals. However, there are many reports of some hard-nosed gamesmanship in the Lone Star State.]

They would drink a lot of beer and they'd be well drunk by the time they played. [Laughs.] It was more heated, more rowdy. Some of it was political. The same people would always win. When Mark went to Crockett I don't think he even placed. But it was fun. At Weiser, that's why it was no fun to sit inside. It was this freezing, air-conditioned gym and everyone just sat there while people scratched through the rounds. In Texas it's outdoors, hot, sweaty, and everyone drinking beer and yelling, sometimes when you're playing, "Yee-hah! Go!" Like the yells in the *Texas Jam Session* album. [See discography.] That's what it was like at [the Weiser] campgrounds.

Another thing that was common in Texas . . . Jerry Thomasson had a lot of kids, seven or eight, and they all had incredible voices. So another thing you'd hear in the campgrounds was Jerry's kids singing these incredible harmonies with his wife Sandra. They sing something on *Texas Jam Session.* They are great people.

SP: Was Benny Thomasson known and respected down there?

MiO: He was like a king in Texas amongst the fiddle people. It's a shame, but the new generation of people at Weiser didn't get a chance to know Benny. I haven't been back to Weiser in a long time. I'm kind of scared to go back, because I remember the influence of Benny and Texas Shorty. I can't imagine it without the original Texas players. For the kids of Mark's age, Benny was a present factor.

SP: Through Mark, Benny will remain known.

MiO: I hope.

I remember one summer we went all around to contests. Buddy Spicher held a contest. We went to a couple in Virginia and the Kentucky State contest. I won three contests in my division that summer. [In 1976 Michelle won in West Virginia, Tennessee, and New Mexico.]

SP: You played in the Texas style?

MiO: Yes. I always used to play [thinking hard, with longer and longer pauses between each remembered title] . . . "Clarinet Polka," . . . "Sopping the Gravy," . . . "Jack of Diamonds," . . . "Fisher's Hornpipe," . . . "Ookpik Waltz." [Laughs.] I never played "Mark's Waltz" [her brother's composition].

Mark and his sister Michelle after his first win in the Open at Weiser, June 1979.

SP: Would Mark play the same tunes through the summer?

MiO: In one summer maybe. He never played the **same.** He would work his rounds out for Weiser and he had to have like 18 songs. Every other contest he would enter was like two rounds.

SP: Can you remember any embarrassing or wacky moments?

MiO: I can tell you one thing that embarrassed Mom. On our first trip to Nashville, I think Mark was 12 years old. We knew Tut Taylor from the Woodenville contest, and he was the only person we knew in town. He sent us over to the Picking Parlor, where Charley Collins and Oswald played. It used to be the hot spot for bluegrass. They're going, "Oh, God, another one of those kids!" They put him on the last number of their set.

You could see the looks on their faces. "This kid can play!" During the break they called up a bunch of people in town and, when the second set began, Vassar Clements, Doctor Perry Harris [one of the founders of Nashville's Grand Masters contest], and a lot of people were there.

Doctor Harris invited him to the Opry a couple of nights later. Mark was wearing cut-off hole-y jeans with threads hanging down his legs, and loose leather sandals. He looked frumpy. Roy Acuff heard him play and decided he was putting him on the Opry. On the Opry everybody's dressed to the hilt, and out comes momma's boy in cut-offs. Mom had no idea he would play. He played "Sally Goodin" and got a standing ovation.

SP: That's amazing from that audience.

MiO: He played an encore number [very rare at the Opry]. To get two songs was a really big thing. For Mom that was embarrassing. I didn't have Mark's stage presence. I was always a nervous wreck. I'd get up there to play and I'd be shaking. I was aware of every person in the audience looking at me. He gets in his own world and creates his own reality.

SP: He probably came home with a bunch of money at the end of the summer.

MiO: Yeah, but it hardly even paid for the trip we had to take there. The Grand Masters paid $1,000. The Juniors at Weiser paid $400 and you were there the whole week. It wasn't exactly a living. [Laughs.] It helped him get started because our parents paid [expenses] and he saved what he made.

I did this from about '72 or '73 to '83, but I didn't enter the last few years. We'd see the same friends every year and hang out. You're watching people grow up . . . who's going to be a pair by Saturday night. Then you didn't see anyone for another year.

Seattle, Washington, August 13, 1990

1979

At 17 years of age, Mark started to go for the big bucks, sacrificing some spontaneity and freedom. Instead, he set about to establish a new, higher criterion of clean, driving contest fiddling.

MO: The third phase comes full circle back to a more straightforward approach to the music. Its arrangements were not as threatening to an old-time purist. [Quoted from the liner notes of the album of the music contained in this book]

He won.

The 1979 Grand National Champions (left to right): Vivian Williams (5th), Dick Barrett (2nd), Mark O'Connor (1st), Junior Daugherty (3rd), Shelly Ann Clark (4th). (Photo courtesy of Stark Photography, Weiser, Idaho)

Grey Eagle 2

The slides in measures 2, 4, 6, and 10 are relatively slow, not the flicks usually notated by a diagonal arrow.

Mention should be made of a characteristic phrase-ending maneuver that Mark inherited from Benny Thomasson. In this piece it appears in measures 8, 24, and 48. It consists of fingering a G♯ or A, then, in the same bow stroke, sounding a double A note.

Section II of this version was not included in "Grey Eagle 1." I first heard Kenny Baker play this strain.

The tempo of "Grey Eagle 2" is MM = 112.

Grey Eagle 2

Mark's first performance with jazz violinist Stephane Grappelli in San Francisco, September 1979.

Leather Britches

Mark stays in third position from measure 33 through part of 51. Though all the notes from measure 41 on can be played in first position, the bowing pattern would be virtually impossible to duplicate. This would greatly change the rhythmic feel of these passages. Third position also allows an open G drone if you desire.

The tempo is MM = 111.

$$\mathbf{\mathtt{C}} \ \| \ G \quad G/B \ | \ C \quad C\sharp^\circ \ | \ G \quad G/B \ | \ D7 \ |$$

$$| \ G \quad G/B \ | \ C \quad C\sharp^\circ \ | \ D7 \quad E\flat 7/B\flat \ | \ D7/A \quad G \ \|$$

Leather Britches

Don't Let the Deal Go Down

"Don't Let the Deal Go Down" is a Texas restructuring of a traditional vocal tune. Except for Section III, Mark handles it as a G version of "Herman's Rag." He plays this at the surprisingly slow tempo of 107.

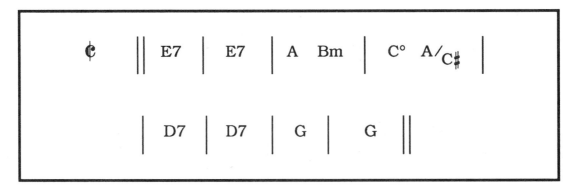

Don't Let the Deal Go Down

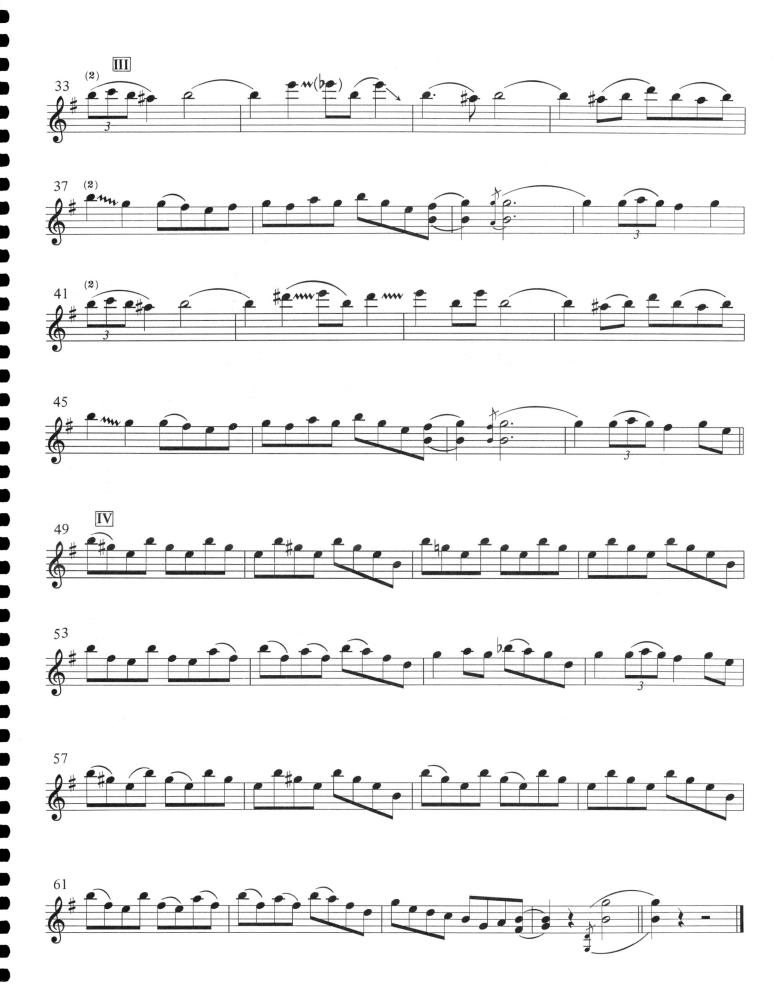

1980

This year was the second of Mark's three consecutive Open Division victories. At this time he was touring with the David Grisman Quintet. He joined as a guitarist (Darol Anger was the violinist).

Left to right: Dick Barrett, Loretta Brank, Mark, Ricky Boen, John Francis, Top 5 finalists in the Open. June 1980.

Golden Eagle Hornpipe

This is a tune that Benny Thomasson rescued from obscurity, learning it from *Cole's 1000 Fiddle Tunes.* He played it with a G♮ in the second measure of the second section (over an Em chord). As you may note, American hornpipes are filled with arpeggios.

The triplets in measures 8 and 40 are probably played with an up bow, allowing a downstroke on the following downbeat. The tempo is MM = 123.

I					
¢ ‖	G6 Am	G∕B B♭°	Am7	D7	
	G6 Am7	G∕B B♭°	Am7 D7	G6 ‖	

II				
B7 B7∕A	E∕G♯ E	A7 A7∕G	D7∕F♯ D7	
C · C♯°	G E7	A7 D7	G ‖	

127

Golden Eagle Hornpipe

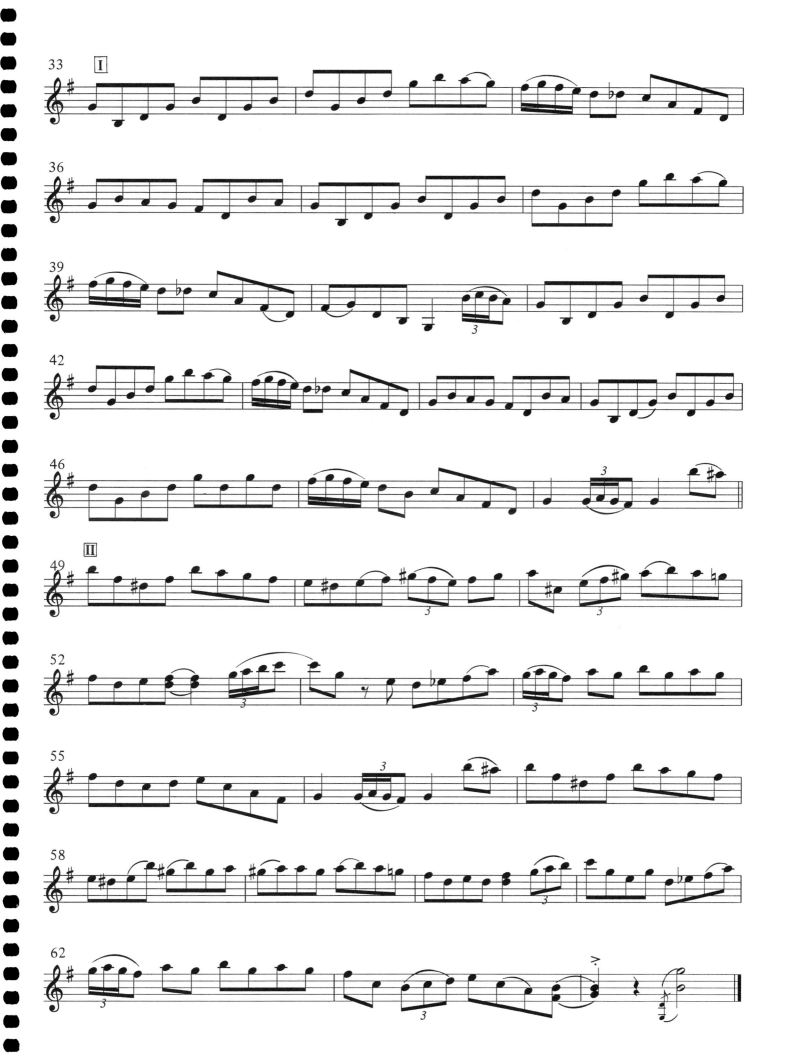

I Don't Love Nobody 2

Mark returns to the original fiddle key of C for this version of "I Don't Love Nobody." Section IV (Section III in "Nobody 1") is now sky high, with a devilishly difficult double-stop in measure 44. The old minor section (III) has also been resuscitated.

One of the contest's emcees, Jack Link, was always gleefully floored by Mark's virtuosity. You can hear his amazed "Wow!" as the last note ends. Other favorite expressions punctuating Mark's efforts include "holy cows" and "mackerels."

The tempo is MM = 121.

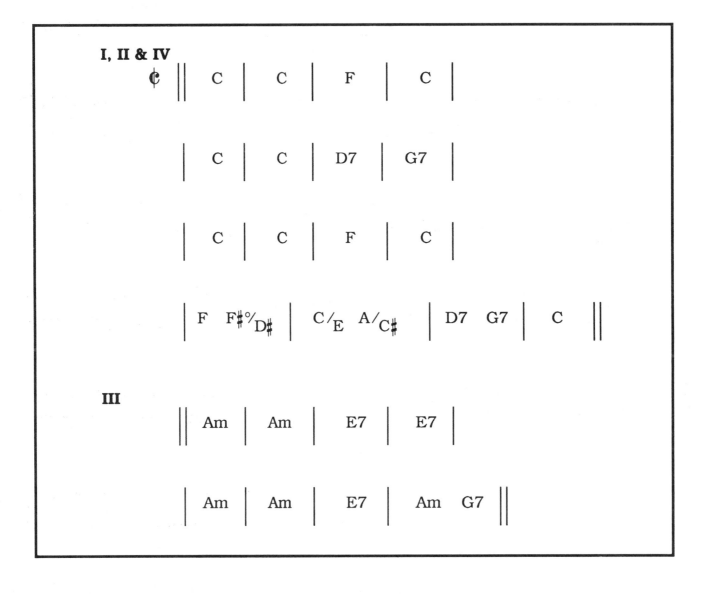

Mark and Benny Thomasson fiddling with accompaniment from Ralph McGraw and Wild Bill Lyle, June 1980.

I Don't Love Nobody 2

Brilliancy 2

"Brilliancy" is quite similar to a Southeast tune known as "Drunken Billy Goat" or "Wild Mountain Goat." This rendition is quite similar to the first version, but quicker at MM = 117.

Brilliancy 2

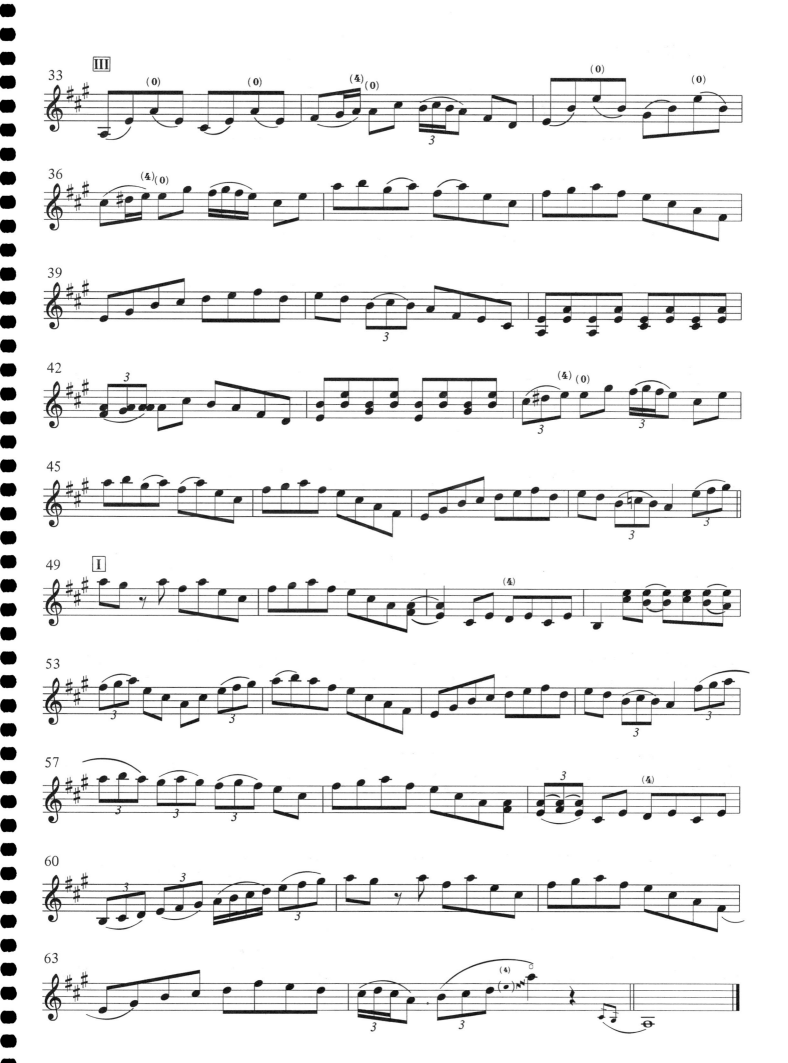

Tugboat

To the untrained ear, "Tugboat" sounds suspiciously like "Sally Johnson." One of the identifying phrases can be found in measures 9 and 57. The tempo is MM = 117.

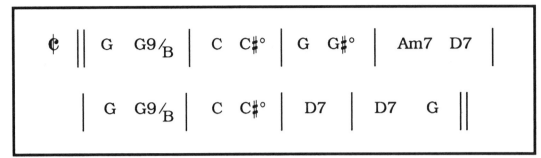

Tugboat

137

Grey Eagle 3

This version of "Grey Eagle" has the same sections as the second version, but in a slightly different order. I associate the first-finger slide in measures 6, 10, and 69 with Howdy Forrester's arrangement, though it is possible that Forrester ultimately got this idea during his stay in Texas.

Mark played this at MM = 121.

Grey Eagle 3

139

Beaumont Rag

In 1980 Mark apparently kept his rags short, possibly to avoid the temptation they offered to run wild. This is a relatively sedate performance, but it is right on the money.

The emcee howls another "Wow, there it is!" Chalk up another first place for Mr. O'Connor. The tempo is MM = 121.

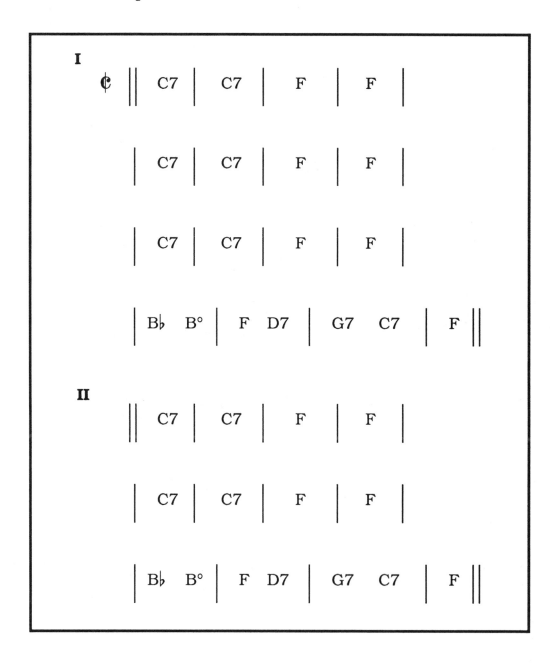

Beaumont Rag

1981

This year Mark was playing with The Dregs, a high-intensity, all-instrumental rock fusion band that featured some heavyweight soloists. He managed some time off to rush to Weiser, and proceeded, with almost no preparation, to become the first competitor to win the Open three years in a row.

Mark's attitude might be summed up by a quote from this period:

MO: You want to play as clean as possible. I mean super clean. Every note. I'd be mad at myself if I played one note that passed by. Every note right on top of the beat . . . . It's better to play a simpler tune, well, not necessarily simpler but one that doesn't go as many places, and play it, man, right down the line. Like crash it. [Quoted from *Contest Fiddling* by Stacy Phillips]

The 1981 Grand Champion Division, left to right: Dale Morris (3rd place), Mark (1st), Loretta Brank (5th), Ricky Boen (4th), Dick Barrett (2nd, not pictured). (Courtesy Stark Photography, Weiser, Idaho)

Hell Among the Yearlings

This is another tune Mark got from Benny Thomasson, who probably got it, in turn, from Clark Kessinger, a great Southeastern fiddler with whom Benny corresponded. Kessinger's rhythmic vagaries have been ironed out, and Mark has put together another beautiful arrangement. For example, Kessinger plays measure 28 just like 27 while, here, the second measure is double-timed. In addition, beginning at measure 49, Section II is played an octave higher than usual.

Years ago, on WWVA Radio in West Virginia, Sleepy Norman, "Your Music Foreman," used to introduce this tune as "Heck Among the Yearlings." Things have loosened up a bit since then.

Mark played this at MM = 121.

Hell Among the Yearlings

Bill Cheatum

With the shorter time limit, Mark began to include two-part tunes not ordinarily part of the Texas-style contest "book." "Bill Cheatum" was popularized by Arthur Smith, an influential Tennessee fiddler who played for a short while in Texas around the same time that Benny Thomasson was creating the style upon which Mark expanded.

Play this at MM = 118.

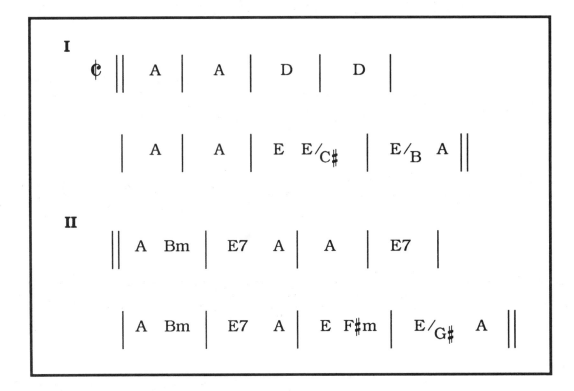

Mark accepting the Winner's Trophy in the Open for the third time in a row.

Bill Cheatum

Sally Goodwin 2

This version of "Sally Goodwin" includes a couple of sections that were omitted in the first rendition. The "(x)" notation in measure 73 indicates some ghosted notes on the way to the harmonic E on the E string in fourth hand position.

Mark played this at MM = 119.

Sally Goodwin 2

Herman's Rag 3

Neither Mark nor I could decide whether the C in measure 26 was meant to be sharp or natural. Use your own artistic judgment. The tempo is MM = 120.

See "Billy in the Lowground" for an explanation of "♩" in measure 15.

Herman's Rag 3

1984

After Mark's win in 1981, contest rules were amended to disqualify three-time winners from competition for one year. So, in 1982 Mark was a judge — of over 300 contestants! He entered and finished second in 1983, but decided not to include any performances from that year.

There were now so many people copying his innovations that Mark decided to come up with a few surprises in 1984, changing the keys of a few tunes, as is described in this chapter.

1978 and 1984 contain my favorite Mark arrangements. He retired from the contest circuit following this victory.

The 1984 Grand National Champions (left to right): John Francis (5th), Ricky Boen (4th), Mark O'Connor (1st), Ricky Turpin (2nd), Tony Ludiker (3rd). (Photo courtesy of Stark Photography, Weiser, Idaho)

Choctaw

"Choctaw" is a rare tune from the Southwest. Its few F notes are sharped (instead of the expected F♮). This raised fourth is a characteristic of Mark's playing in the key of C. He played this at MM = 114.

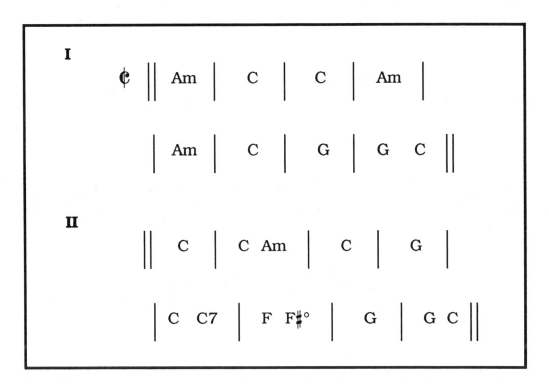

155

Choctaw

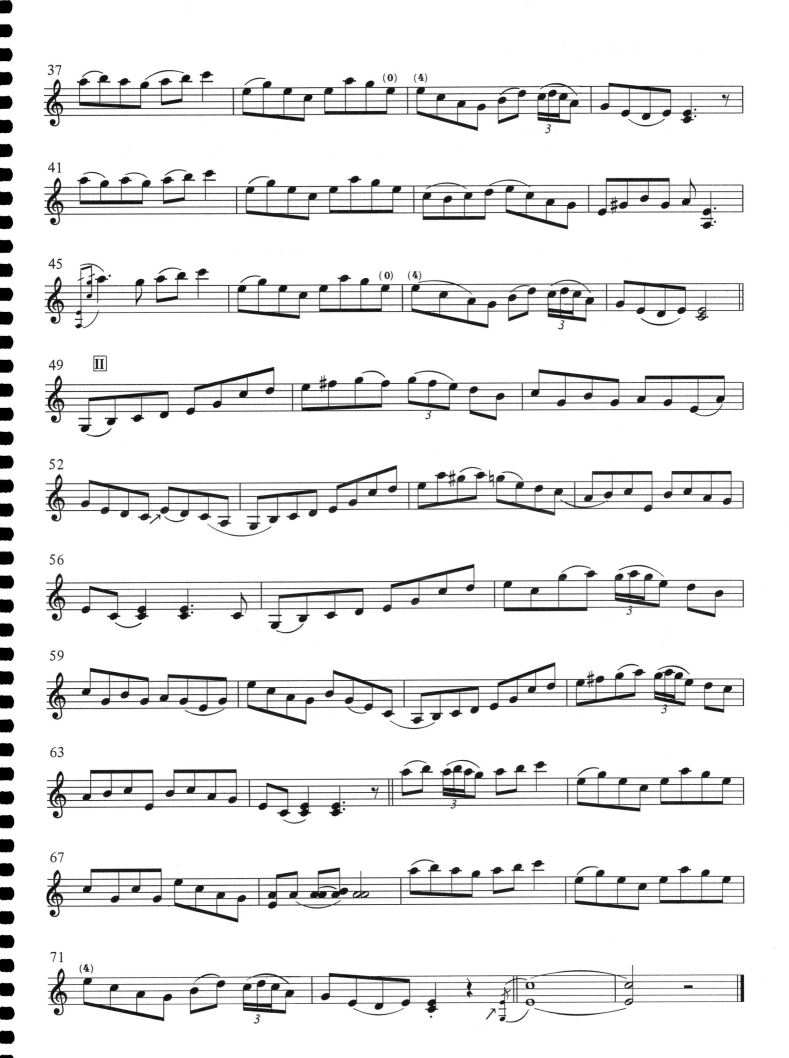

Westphalia Waltz

"Westphalia Waltz" is always done in the key of G. In my mind's eye I can see the hordes of O'Connor clones diving for their tape recorders when it was announced that Mark was going to play it in the key of F. The new setting allows some fun double-stops in measures 10–16, 29, 39, and 43–45 — in other words, most of the tune.

Mark's waltz tempo has decreased to MM = 110.

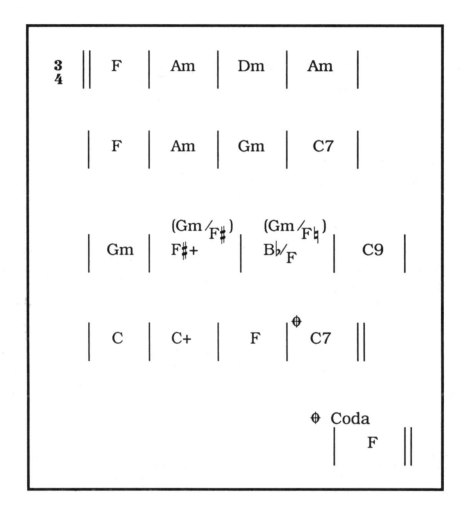

The recording room at Weiser, where the latest licks are taped and then learned over the winter. June 1984.

Westphalia Waltz

Black and White Rag 2

"Black and White Rag" in the key of D — Mark obviously had some free time while hanging out in Nashville to come up with this idea! Section I is a killer, with Mark's fingering setting up some exacting bow rocking. Section II is in a lower register than its equivalent in "Black and White Rag 1," until the challenging run in measures 45–46.

Mark played this at MM = 113.

I

¢ ‖ A | A | D | D |

| A | A | D | D |

| A | A | D | D |

| B7 | E7 | A7 | D ‖

II

‖ G | E7 | A | A |

| D7 | D7 | G E7 | A7 D7 |

| G | E7 | A | A |

| D | D | D | G ‖

161

Black and White Rag 2

Herman's Hornpipe

"Herman's Hornpipe" is another tune that I have heard only contest fiddlers perform. Mark's rendition is a demanding exercise in bowing. He played this at MM = 114.

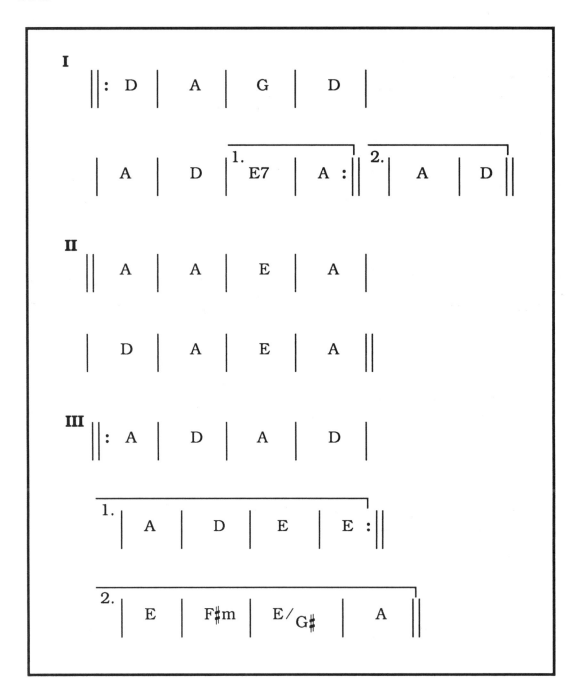

An interior shot of the Weiser Fiddlers' Hall of Fame   *(Courtesy Stark Photography, Weiser, Idaho)*

Herman's Hornpipe

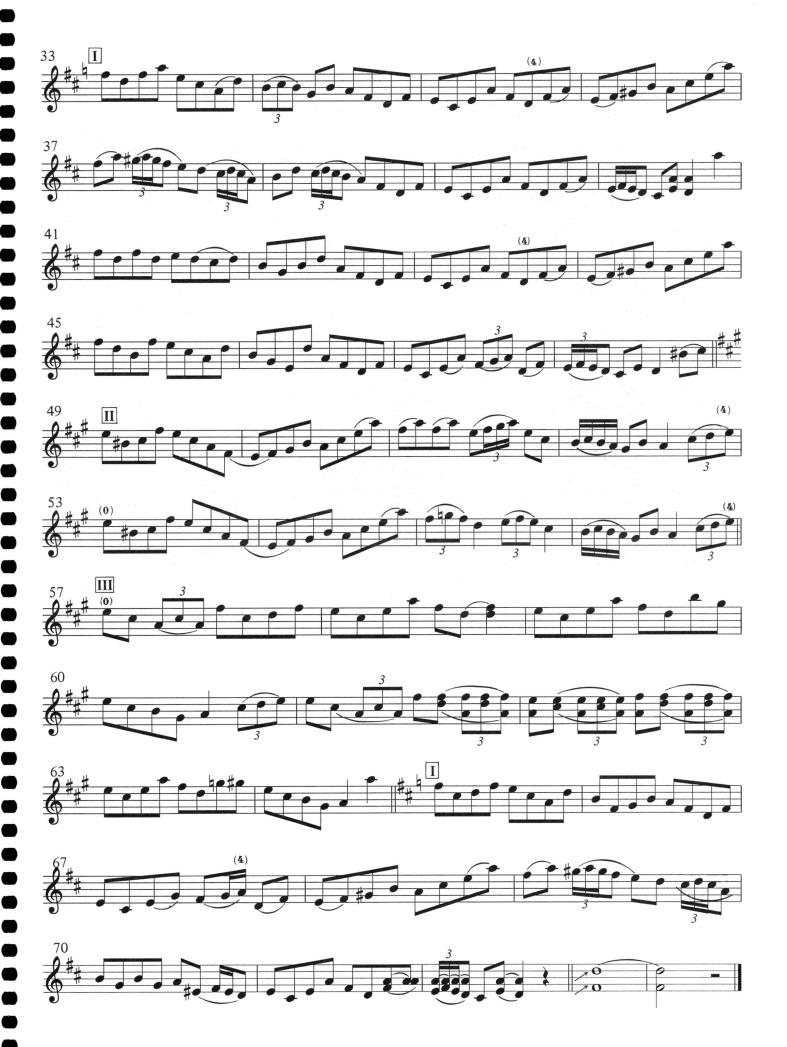

Mark at Weiser, June 1984.

Dill Pickle Rag 2

Next, Mark changes the setting of "Dill Pickle" from the standard G to C and adds the third section that was omitted in "Dill Pickle 1." My favorite lick is the one over the D7 chord in measures 59–60. It does not hurt to have big hands. This performance warrants a "Holy mackerel!" from Jack Link.

Mark played this at MM = 112.

I

¢ ‖: C | C | D7 | D7 |

| G F9/A | B♭° B° | 1. C A/C♯ | D7 G7 :‖

2. | G B° | C ‖

II

‖: G7 | C | G7 | C ‖

| G7 | C | 1. D7 | G :‖ 2. | D7 G7 | C C7 ‖

III

‖ F | F | B♭ | F |

| F Am/E | Dm F♯° | G G7 | C C7 |

| F | F | B♭ | F |

| B♭ B° | F D7 | G7 C7 | F ‖

Dill Pickle Rag 2

When Mark would prepare for the next round, a crowd would gather and tape recorders would appear. June 1984.

Sally Ann

This is one of those deceptively simple-sounding tunes that Mark mentions in the interview. Mark plays this at MM = 116, as near perfection as anyone could ask.

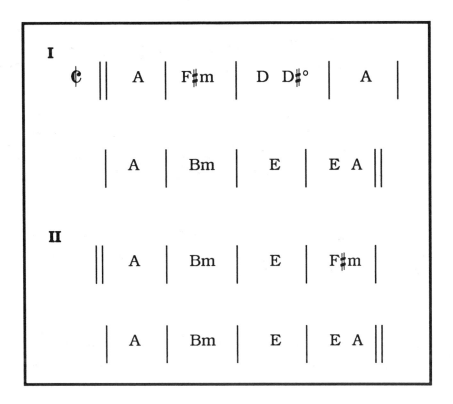

Sally Ann

Grandfather Polka 3

Mark returns this tune to the original clarinet key of B♭, jumps into E♭ in Section II, and plays an authentic polka riff with the staccato phrasing in measure 50. The tempo is MM = 112.

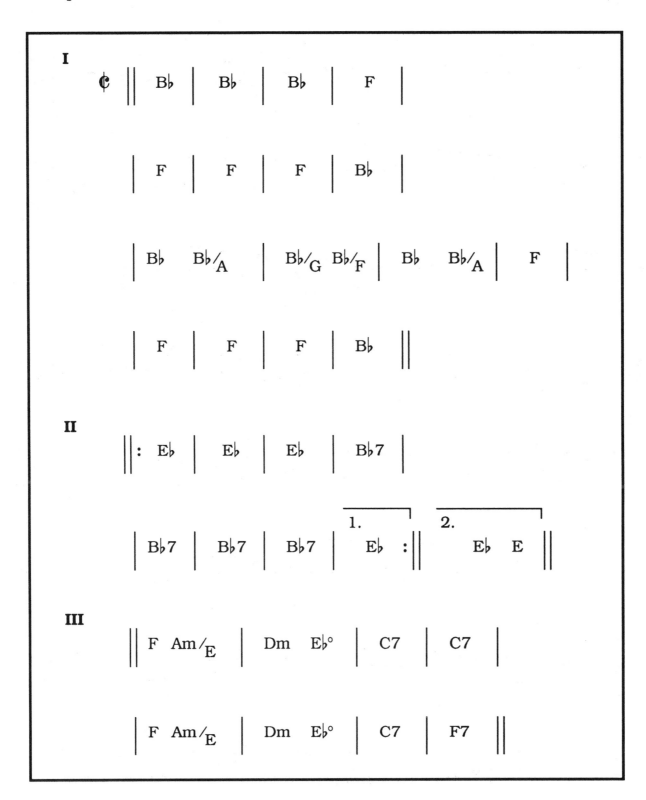

An interior shot of the Weiser Fiddlers' Hall of Fame.   (Courtesy Stark Photography, Weiser, Idaho)

Grandfather Polka 3

Mark at Weiser getting ready for the Saturday night finals, June 1984.

Arkansas Traveller

This most standard of standards is a good vehicle for the comparison of Mark's approach with other American styles. It is obviously the same tune, but the clichéd runs have been mutated to something fresh. As usual, Mark has conceived an interesting third-position strain.

The tempo is MM = 121.

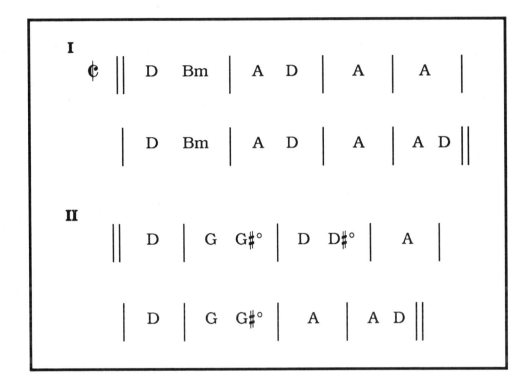

Arkansas Traveller

Jesse Polka

"Jesse Polka" is derived from the Mexican tune "Jesusito en Chihuahua." For his final tune-of-choice, Mark chose to transpose from the standard G to the key of A.

SP: Any reason for picking a particular new key?

MO: I probably went through a couple of obvious keys. It could have been just one lick. One part of the tune might have felt real neat in a certain key. There were a couple of double-stop things that went along with the melody that felt really natural.

Check out the great riff in measures 41–48. Mark played this at a tempo of MM = 118.

With a final "Holy mackerel!" Mark exited to cheers and one more Open victory.

I ¢ ‖ A | A | A | E |

| E | E | E | A |

| A | A | A | D |

| D D♯° | A F♯7 | B7 E7 | A ‖

II ‖ A | A | E | A |

| A | A | E | A ‖

III ‖ B7 | E | B7 | E |

| B7 | E | B7 | E ‖

(Photo courtesy of Stark Photography, Weiser, Idaho)

Jesse Polka

The Guitar Accompaniment

In the American Southwest of the 1930s and '40s, the dominant commercial music was Western swing. This featured a wide-ranging repertoire, including old-time fiddle tunes played with a swing rhythm section. Eldon Shamblin, guitarist for the Bob Wills band, evolved a particularly pleasing moving-bass line accompaniment that was adapted by the guitarists who backed fiddlers in local contests.

As played presently, it involves the use of "sock" chords (chord shapes without open strings) and the inclusion of passing chords implied by the bass lines. The pattern usually consists of a pluck of a bass note followed by a strum of the chord. When there is one chord in a measure, pluck the root note on beat 1, and the fifth note of the chord on beat 3 (counting in the cut-time meter used in this book). For example, the rhythm pattern indicated by ₵ |A| is (in bass clef)

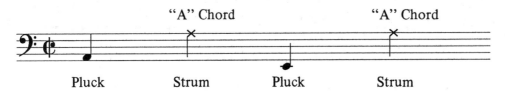

The chords that Mark has chosen are just one possibility out of the many acceptable patterns for each tune. In fact, the progression is usually varied by the accompanists during a single rendition. Occasionally, I have given alternate chords in parentheses.

Any letters beneath a slash indicate a particular bass note. So ₵ | E E/G♯ | means to play two beats of an E with an E note in the bass, then two beats of E with a G♯ in the bass.

Slash lines **above** the chord notation indicate the number of beats when that is not obvious in context. So,

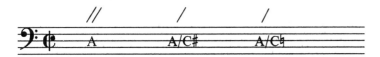

means to play two beats of an A chord with A in the bass, then one beat apiece with C♯, then C♮ in the bass. In cut-time meter, just pluck these last two notes, since there is no time to strum the chords.

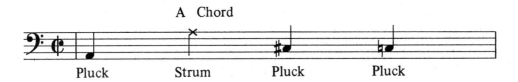

Matt Glaser Interview

Matt Glaser is the head of the jazz string department at the Berklee School of Music in Boston, Massachusetts. He is currently working on his Master's thesis in ethnomusicology at Tufts University, titled "Controlled Improvisation in Texas Contest Style Fiddling: Mark O'Connor and Benny Thomasson play 'Grey Eagle.'" Having been involved with this kind of music as both player and academician, he has some unique insights into its workings.

Stacy Phillips: What is meant when people say that Texas fiddling uses a long bow?

Matt Glaser: [Laughs.] I don't know **what** the hell they're talking about. I think it's because the style is smoother in some ways than bluegrass or Appalachian playing. I don't think anyone uses a lot of slurs [in this style].

SP: It sounds like long bows because the bow changes are so smooth.

MG: It must be something like that.

SP: Can you make some comparisons between Mark and Benny's bowing?

MG: I was struck by how dynamic, in the musical sense, Benny's bowing was. In listening to these tapes of Benny [in the 1950s], he carves this stuff out . . . lots of rises and falls in the volume. [He sings a couple of phrases imitating Benny, with many volume shifts of just a few eighth notes in duration.] Mark pointed this out as I was listening with him . . . laying into certain notes differently over a line. Also, he had a kind of "chugga-chugga" feeling [in the bowing] which I really like. I think Mark sort of smoothed that out of his playing. Benny was rougher in a way that I think is really great . . . "chugga-chugga." Early Mark had some of that. For me, Mark's bowing is indivisible from his cosmic coordination and rhythm . . . this seamless, flawless, unbelievably perfect technical thing, which I find freaky.

SP: Freaky?

MG: It freaks me out to listen to it. How could this be? How can someone play with this kind of technical perfection?

SP: Did Benny use the sharp 4 note as much as Mark? "Grey Eagle" in the key of A is one key they don't do that.

MG: You'll find in modal tunes, when the line is going up, they'll use a ♯4 in like Indian music, and a ♮4 in the line coming down. I think I've noticed some of that with Benny. It's not an iron-clad rule.

SP: The ♯4 acts as a leading tone to the 5 note, and on the way down you don't have that sort of pull.

MG: Right. You have a half step one way or the other. On the way down, you have the half step from 4 to 3, and on the way up from the ♯4 to the 5.

SP: Mark thought it also had something to do with how your hand lays.

MG: Yeah, that may be in keys like C or G, certainly.

SP: He felt uncomfortable doing it in A.

MG: Your hand is higher up on the neck and there's a bigger stretch between the first and third fingers. I'm sure there must be physical reasons for a lot of this stuff.

SP: Anything else you'd like to say about Mark's playing?

MG: I haven't done any writing yet [for his thesis]. My focus is on individual creativity in that style and how both Mark and Benny are incredibly creative in different ways. I haven't figured it out exactly . . . how these guys can play certain phrases many, many different times, always keeping the basic shape intact and yet doing a lot of little different things each time. That's what blows my mind about this. It's obvious when I play this idiom that I'm faking it. There's strict adherence to this core melody . . . it's sort of organic. They don't have to think about it much, and they can always spin off of it.

I have eight or nine versions of these two guys playing this one tune, and there are certain phrases where they never play the exact same thing. You'd think that there would be certain phrases, at least two of the eight times they might play the exact same thing. But there are eight different phrases. Yet the shape of the line is always the same, and the overall meaning, the gestalt if you will [laughs], of the line is always the same somehow.

SP: I'm going to like using that word in this book.

MG: You don't want to make me appear too intelligent if at all possible.

I'm trying not to force myself to come to any particular conclusions [in the thesis] except to examine the fact that these two guys are specific individuals who are creative within a tradition. A lot of ethnomusicology doesn't look at individuals. It looks at some social or group movement.

Especially, Benny to me was like Bach . . . Mark maybe like Mozart. I'm not sure if that's an apt analogy.

I'm also interested in contest fiddling . . . in the sort of three levels that help to make these people such great players. One is individual practice time, like Benny sitting at home in his bathroom working on tunes.

[Benny Thomasson: I've lost a lot of crops playing the fiddle. (Laughs.) I've stayed in the bathroom sometimes all night, working on one tune, getting it to where it'd be presentable. Better than last year. (From *Contest Fiddling* by Stacy Phillips)]

Another is the jam sessions where everyone gets to take off a little bit. Each person takes a good long whack at the tune, and they go round in a circle so there's a competitive thing, but with no repercussions if you stretch yourself out. Then you have to boil everything down for the contests.

So there are these three different scenarios that force you to keep getting better. They double back upon one another. You know you're going to go to the contest, so you keep working on the tune by yourself at home. Then you want to get together with other guys you're going to be in the contest with and play in a more informal setting. So it works to keep things at a high level.

I talked to Junior Daugherty [a perennial high finisher at Weiser during Benny's and Mark's appearances there] about this. He was saying that now it's gotten bad. The kids won't play with one another. They don't want to give away their variations. There's this ultra-competitiveness. It used to be, when it was Junior, Benny, Texas Shorty, maybe Herman Johnson . . . they were always hanging out together with less of this high pressure.

SP: How about the melodic aspects of what Mark did compared to the style he learned from Benny? Mark had several stages.

MG: Benny was fond of doing stuff over two octaves. That's another reason he sort of reminds me of Bach . . . as opposed to it all happening within one octave. In the course of eight bars of the high variation of "Grey Eagle," he'd go all the way down [to the G string]. Mark did that when he started. [See the first 16 measures of "Grey Eagle 1."] Then he got more into keeping the variations in one octave. His variations would all be in the high octave but with a greater degree of melodic variation.

SP: More twisting around . . .

MG: . . . than Benny would do . . . jazzier in a sense. Benny did a lot more rhythmic jumps, hops and skips. Mark was able to do more complicated turns.

I have all these computer printouts of the 8-bar phrases [from "Grey Eagle"], 12 different ways Mark plays the opening section, comparing the first 8 bars with the second 8 bars, which should be identical, but aren't. It's interesting to see how they vary the second 8 bars. Generally they get more out . . . more chromatic stuff.

Cambridge, Mass., August 27, 1990

The following chart is excerpted from Matt's forthcoming thesis. It compares the first 8 measures with the second 8 measures of six different renditions of "Grey Eagle" as played by Mark O'Connor. The first version was played at the Ashokan, New York fiddle camp, and the second at the Berkshire Mountain Bluegrass Festival. The next two versions correspond to "Grey Eagle" 1 and 2 in this book. (Note that there are a few differences in Matt's and my transcriptions.) The fifth arrangement is from Mark's early album *Pickin' in the Wind* (Rounder 0068), and the last is a third offering from Weiser that is "Grey Eagle 3."

Mark O'Connor

This chart is reprinted by permission of Matt Glaser.

"A" Section

Discography and Bibliography

Here is a list of Mark O'Connor's solo records and a couple of books I have written that you might find interesting:

Mark O'Connor — National Junior Fiddle Champion (Rounder 0046)
Pickin' in the Wind (Rounder 0068)
Markology (Rounder 0090)
On the Rampage (Rounder 0188)
Soppin' the Gravy (Rounder 0137)
False Dawn (Rounder 0165)
Meanings of (Warner Bros.)
Stone From Which the Ark Was Made (Warner Bros. 25539)
Elysian Forest (Warner Bros. 25736)
On the Mark (Warner Bros. 25970)
The New Nashville Cats (Warner Bros.)
Mark O'Connor — The Championship Years (Country Music Foundation 015)

Contest Fiddling by Stacy Phillips (Mel Bay Publications 93940): This book contains transcriptions and in-depth analyses of the Texas fiddle style that Mark popularized. Featured fiddlers include Benny Thomasson, Jim "Texas Shorty" Chancellor, Dick Barrett, Junior Daugherty, Howdy Forrester, Byron Berline, and some tunes by Mark that are not included in this book.

Bluegrass Fiddle Styles by Stacy Phillips and Kenny Kosek (Oak Pub. 000185)
Western Swing Fiddle by Stacy Phillips (Oak Pub.)

These books are available from me at 36 Cromwell Hill Road, Monroe, NY 10950.

Epilogue — Looking Ahead

Stacy Phillips: Talk about the things you've recently recorded. They're quite a departure.

Mark O'Connor: It's composing. I get to make up exactly what's in my head and make an album of it. It hasn't had anything to do with a style of music, what people expect of me, or a marketing ploy. I was going, "I like this," not picking tunes that other people might like. All my personal albums have been like that.

Right now I'm working on a country fiddle extravaganza record [*The New Nashville Cats*] . . . writing fiddle tunes in different styles of country music.

[Regarding a recent promotional tour he had done for his latest album, I mentioned that I had heard that he had not performed any fiddle tunes on the shows.]

I was trying to break into a jazz market . . . to cater to a certain crowd — jazz radio stations, who were like the judges. At Weiser the judge is from South Dakota and he's about 62 years old and he likes Midwestern old-time fiddling. So I'm going to play "Hell Among the Yearlings" and "Bill Cheatum" as best I can. [For the album promotion] I wanted to give a good all-around contemporary jazz-fusion show.

If I was playing shows regularly for the love of playing, I would mix it up a lot more. I grew up fiddling old-time music. I can almost do it in my sleep. I'm giving myself a stretch all the time.

SP: It takes time for the audience to catch up.

MO: I have different audiences. Once I had different outlets [like Grisman and The Dregs], I didn't have to stretch fiddle tunes. [With Grisman] I could stretch as far as I could, and it wasn't enough. I was going, "This is what I've been looking for!" I didn't have someone at my shoulder saying, "Now get back! No, you're going too far!" People were saying, "Go for more! Not enough, man!" I felt humble and almost humiliated. Nobody said, "You're too fancy. You're too good."

With The Dregs it was "Play as fast as you can! As fast as your fingers can move is the goal here!" [Laughter.]

Now I can approach old-time music playing close to the melody. It's all hard. When somebody says, "That must not be as hard to do as your 'Sally Johnson' at 14" . . . it's a different type of hard. You can always have a more inspired performance . . . more tone, more in tune. The goal changed. I grew and learned appropriateness. I had a lot of fun playing the old-time tunes. Music is communication. I have to communicate with my audience to have a good time.

Being in Nashville is a different kind of controversy. Some people here thought I was a classical violinist, or that I was playing too progressive again! And being pegged a bluegrass player, which is a no-no in country music. Some people thought I was too jazzy. This was all happening at once! Explain that!

SP: Eventually they changed their minds, because now you're all over the place.

Mark and his son Forrest, June 1990   *(Photo by Jim McGuire)*

MO: [In the studio] you always have to be on your toes because you're only as good as your last performance. [Laughs.] I hope one day there'll be enough people that like what I do and go through the changes that I go through with me.

If I can influence people to want to learn the fiddle because of the way I play it, that would be a positive thing. It's a gain in the fiddle community. That's why I listed all the fiddlers who influenced me. I wanted to make sure the people listening to me knew, if they wanted to find out what makes Mark O'Connor tick, they should research these people. It's a respect for tradition.

[I compared Benny Thomasson's and Tommy Jarrell's styles and influence on younger fiddlers.]

MO: There's no substitute for tradition. It would be a sad world if there was not someone to carry that on. Hopefully there are fans who would say, "Forget Mark O'Connor! Tommy Jarrell, that's where it's at. I'm going to devote my musical life to him." I say "Great," because someone needs to carry on that tradition. The whole music world needs that.

SP: What do you listen to these days?

MO: I don't have the time to really listen. I just check out stuff . . . a lot of classical, Bach, Mozart, and Haydn. I'm actually getting enthused about fiddling again . . . looking at different angles to approach fiddling. I'm listening as if I'm playing it. The way my mind works, I hear a melody in my head and it's almost as if I've played it.

SP: You're fingering it in your head.

MO: Yes. Some of it sounds best if I keep it in my head [laughs], like the Bach, because I don't have the training.

That's the first step towards coming into your own as a musician . . . imagining the possibility of being able to play a certain way. When I was 11 or 12, I had a feeling of what it was like to play at the level of Benny Thomasson. It wasn't like I had to practice the proper [left] wrist. I could imagine the perfect posture and how it would allow my fourth finger more freedom. I didn't have to practice to imagine the goal.

I didn't do everything to be like Benny. I assembled information in my head about the different aspects of what I would like to pick up to get better. There's a certain amount you can do without the instrument at all.

SP: [After listening to a cut from his country-oriented album.] When you get down to it, avoiding over-analysis, you're a terrific musician. You seem to be pushing your limits, driven to expand and make yourself better.

MO: I'm something of a mad [pause] man. [Laughs.]

It's been a revelation to listen to the tape [of the music in this book]. Even though it's not that long ago, I'd forgotten what playing in the earlier contests was like. I've graduated through so many musical phases since then. I've learned a lot about myself that I'd forgotten. The intensity is there from the beginning . . . always searching for the place I wasn't at yet.

Nashville, June 12–13, 1990